*To my bubby Sadie Pechenick
who helped to provide me
with my Jewish "neshama"*

Contents

Acknowledgments

While there are many who have helped me to shape the enormous quantity of Jewish law with insights from Jewish tradition and community custom, I particularly want to thank the families of Temple Sholom in Bridgewater, New Jersey, who have allowed me to share life cycle events. I also want to thank these collegues who carefully reflected on each nuance of Jewish practice and custom as presented in this book: Rabbis Charles Simon, Barry Cytron, Stephen Lerner, Jack Segal, Joel Zaiman, Dr. Howard Adelman, and Bernice Balter.

I also want to thank Shoshana Zonderman for graciously allowing me to reprint Preparing for Parenthood material.

Preface

Yehudah ben Tema taught:
At five years of age—the study of the Bible;
At ten—the study of the Mishnah;
At thirteen—responsibility for Mitzvot;
At fifteen—the study of Talmud;
At eighteen—marriage;
At twenty—pursuit of a livelihood . .
—Ethics of the Fathers 5:23

"*B*e fruitful and multiply." This is Judaism's first mitzvah, the first commandment in the Bible. In Judaism, having children is not only a religious obligation but undoubtedly one of the crowning achievements in the life of any husband and wife. So many of our Jewish customs and ceremonies are intended primarily for one's children that we can definitely say that the child is the center of any Jewish home. The Passover Seder is structured to impress children through experiential rituals, with the ideal of liberty. Hanukkah, the Festival of Lights; Purim, with its costumes, noisemakers and carnivals; and Lag B'Omer, with its picnics and bonfires—all are principally geared toward children.

And then there are the Jewish life cycle events—*Brit Milah*, the Naming, *Simchat Bat*, *Pidyon HaBen*, *Bar* and *Bat Mitzvah*—all these are special celebrations of children. Each rite is accompanied by a pageantry of ritual and custom, law and folklore, feasting and celebration. Each rite is intended as an opportunity for families to celebrate and rejoice with friends, linking themselves not only to the community of today but to the communities of past generations.

As a Conservative congregational rabbi for almost two decades, I have had the pleasure of sharing these Jewish life cycle events with hundreds of families. From the questions that have been asked of me over these many years, I have come to realize that many parents lack the knowledge they need in order to make the important first decisions to properly prepare for a life cycle event. Few are prepared to make any sort of meaningful decisions. I have often been asked to recommend something they might read to help improve their understanding, and over the years I have made various suggestions. In a number of instances the parents reported that the books they chose to read were "weighty" and that many of the described practices were not applicable to the Conservative Jewish family. Though purchased, many of the books went unread.

Rites of Passage: A Guide to the Jewish Life Cycle is designed with the Conservative Jew in mind. It is intended to provide members of the Conservative movement with an easy-to-read description of the life cycle observances, their historical background, ceremonial customs and rituals that will assist in enhancing their celebration of Jewish rites of passage. It incorporates the important decisions reached by the Rabbinical Assembly Committee on Jewish Law and Standards that help further define the celebration of life cycle events for the Conservative Jew. It also includes several newer ceremonies created to recognize significant events in a Jewish woman's life, including a Jewish Parenting Ceremony and the *Simchat Bat* and *Pidyon HaBat* ceremonies.

I have made every attempt to be mainstream in my presentation, fully aware that there is always likely to be a wider range of opinion and practice in Conservative synagogues than what I have presented here. Remember that if you wish further information or clarification on any of these topics, you should consult your rabbi.

May your celebrations always enhance the Jewishness of your family and help to unite us as a people. I hope that they will help to pave a life for you that will bring added sanctity to your community and an increased desire to walk humbly with your God.

Ronald H. Isaacs
5752

1

Sources of Jewish Law

There are those who would think that we have but two alternatives, to reject or to accept the law, but in either case to treat it as a dead letter. But these alternatives are repugnant to the whole tradition of Judaism, and it is to combat them that the (Jewish Theological) Seminary was brought into being . . . Jewish law must be preserved but . . . it is subject to interpretation by those who have mastered it, and . . . the interpretation placed upon it by duly authorized masters in every generation must be accepted with as much reverence as those which were given in previous generations.

—Professor Louis Finkelstein

*A*ccording to Jewish law, may a newborn be named after a deceased beloved aunt? What is the naming ceremony for a girl? When is a *pidyon haben* not performed? May weddings take place between Passover and Shavuot? When must an unveiling take place?

These questions are typical of questions that are often asked concerning the rites of passage observed by Jews. In order to understand the observances of the important life cycle events, one must be able to distinguish between law, custom, and superstition. Sometimes one can find a local custom which is stringently observed while a basic law is seemingly overlooked. Before beginning a study of the Jewish rites of passage and their rituals, customs, and folklore, a brief analysis of the sources of Jewish law is in order. An understanding of the sources of Jewish practice will help place the laws, customs, traditions, and folklore into their proper perspective, leading to a better appreciation of the beauty of our Jewish rites of passage.

What is the earliest source of Jewish law?

The Torah, sometimes called the *Humash,* Pentateuch, or the Five Books of Moses, is the earliest source of Jewish law. The Torah consists of the books of Genesis, Exodus, Leviticus, Numbers, and Deuteronomy. Reverence for and acceptance of the Torah are the foundation of Jewish law and its interpretation. Although the Torah does contain those guiding principles from which Jewish law and its interpretation spring, it does not contain all of Jewish law. A parallel can be found by comparing the Torah to the United States Constitution. Although the Constitution is a relatively brief document, the shelves of libraries are filled with many thousands of volumes based on it. These books contain additional laws established by legislation and interpreted by courts. Similarly, Jews look to the Torah as authoritative on

many basic traditions, but constantly seek the rabbinic interpretation of the law which followed in order to definitively
learn how to live as authentic Jews.

What is the Talmud?

The Talmud is the major source for the rabbinic interpretation of the law. The Mishnah, which is part of the Talmud
(sometimes called the Oral Law), sought to explain the laws
as set forth in the Torah. It consists of the teachings of
the *tannaim,* scholars and sages who lived prior to 220 C.E.
Judah HaNasi and his associates sifted through, evaluated,
and edited a large number of legal opinions that had been
expressed over the centuries in the learning academies.
The product of their work was the Mishnah, a six-volume
collection of legal opinions.

The Mishnah could neither encompass all the situations
in any person's life nor cover new situations which were
constantly developing. New situations and ambiguities in
the text of the Mishnah often led to discussion among
the rabbis, and soon new rulings and decisions began to
appear. Numerous life experiences, cases presented to the
rabbis, and questions asked of them combined to expand and
elaborate the teachings of the Mishnah. These later teachings
were set down in the Gemara, which was completed around
the year 500 C.E. The scholars whose views are presented
in the discussions of the Gemara are known as the *amoraim,*
meaning "interpreters" or "speakers." For the most part they
lived in Babylonia, where the great academies were situated
following the destruction of the Jerusalem Temple. The
Mishnah and the Gemara together comprise the Talmud,
the major compendium of discussions on Jewish Law held
by the rabbis, and the record of their decisions. The Talmud
also contains Jewish folklore, sayings, and stories.

A second Talmud, the Palestinian or Jerusalem Talmud,

was also composed. The Mishnah of Judah HaNasi is the central text of this work as well. However, the Gemara of the Palestinian Talmud consists of all the discussions that took place among the amoraim in the learning academies in Palestine. The Palestinian Talmud has always enjoyed a lesser status than the Babylonian Talmud because its academies were not equal in stature to those of Babylonia.

For the first five hundred years following the final editing of the Talmud—from the years 500–1000 C.E., great scholars continued the process of interpreting the Bible. They also explained and commented on the Talmud and gained new insights from its teachings. This period is known as the gaonic period, and its scholars are called *geonim* (singular *gaon,* meaning "his eminence"). Among the better known geonim are Hai, Sherira, and Amram, each of whom headed a Babylonian learning academy. These scholars, as well as those who followed after them for approximately the next five centuries, until the mid sixteenth century, were known as the *rishonim,* meaning the "early ones." In addition to analyzing and studying the Talmud, they wrote commentaries on it and answered questions directed to them by rabbis and teachers all over the world. Among the more celebrated scholars of the post-gaonic period (after the year 1000 C.E.) was Jacob of Fez, known as the Alfasi or by the acronym Rif, the French-born Solomon ben Yitzchak, better known by the acronym Rashi and Moses ben Maimon of Spain, also known by the acronym Rambam and by the patronymic Maimonides.

What are the codes?

The Talmud never really served the Jewish people as a code of Jewish traditions and rituals. The sea of Talmud was so vast that it was often difficult for a person to locate all the specific references on any given subject. This situation led the rabbis to begin to codify the laws and set them in order, according to subject matter, so that one would be able to find them more easily. Among the many famous codifiers was Rabbi Moses ben Maimon (Maimonides: 1135–1204). In his fourteen-volume code of law, called the *Mishneh Torah,* Maimonides arranged in a methodical and logical manner the established laws as set forth in the Talmud. The *Mishneh Torah* is still fruitfully studied today.

Other Jews also created their own codes of law. Rabbi Asher ben Jechiel (1250–1320), the spiritual leader of the community of Toledo in Spain, made an abstract of the material in the Talmud. His son, Rabbi Jacob ben Asher, wrote another code, using a method similar to that of Maimonides, that is, arranging the laws by classification rather than by location in the Talmud. He called his work *Arba'ah Turim.* ("The Four Rows"). This compendium of Jewish law consisted of four parts:

- *Orach Chayim,* dealing with laws of prayer and a person's daily conduct.
- *Yoreh Deah,* dealing with the dietary laws, laws of ritual purity and mourning.
- *Even Haezer,* dealing with personal and family matters, including laws of marriage and divorce.
- *Choshen Mishpat,* dealing with criminal and civil law.

By far the most popular, respected, and authoritative code of Jewish law, called the *Shulchan Aruch* ("The Prepared Table"), was written by Rabbi Joseph Karo. The *Shulchan Aruch* is actually an abbreviated and simplified form of the Arba Turim, taking into account the views of previous codifiers, including those of the Alfasi and Maimonides. This code dealt with Jewish law and practice wherever the Jew might be, at home, synagogue, or business. The *Shulchan Aruch*

completed in approximately 1555 and together with subse-
quent commentaries on it became the most authoritative
book of Jewish law and observance. Since Joseph Karo was
a Sephardic scholar, he was charged with ignoring the views
of Ashkenazic (French and German) legal authorities. As a
result, Moses Isserles of Poland, a sixteenth-century scholar
known by the acronym Rama, wrote supplementary notes
to the *Shulchan Aruch* called the *Mappah* ("tablecloth"). The
notes of Isserles set forth the views of Ashkenazic scholars
and presented the customs of their communities. When
Karo and Isserles do not agree on a particular custom, the
Sephardim generally follow Karo while the Ashkenazim will
most often follow Isserles.

With the publication of the *Shulchan Aruch,* the period
of the early scholars (*rishonim*) ended and the period of
the *acharonim,* "the later ones," began. From the end of
the sixteenth century to the present the *acharonim* have
issued authoritative interpretations of the law. Among the
famous *acharonim* are the Polish scholar Solomon Luria,
known by the acronym Maharshal, the Hungarian Moses
Sofer and Rabbi Abraham Kook, the former chief rabbi of
the Ashkenazic community in Palestine in 1921.

A very important late twentieth century interpreter of
Jewish law for the Conservative movement was Rabbi Isaac
Klein (z'l). His *Guide to Jewish Religious Practice* serves as an
important law code for many Conservative Jews (see later in
this chapter).

What are customs, folklore, and superstitions?

Laws and customs are the building blocks of Jewish life,
unifying the community. Whereas a law derives from the
Torah and Talmud, custom derives from popular practice.
It is created by the people, serving the needs of the general
community. Unlike law, which is imposed from without,

custom (*minhag*) takes root and flourishes from within. For example, when reciting the prayer the *Shema* some communities have the custom of standing during its recitation while others follow the custom of staying seated. In a second example, Jews in Israel follow their custom of observing fewer days of some festivals (e.g., Sukkot, Passover, Shavuot) than do Diaspora Jews. Many life cycle rituals are not based on the regulations of the Bible or Talmud, but are simply customs, the unique practice of a ritual by a large number of Jews in a community.

Folklore refers to the creative, spiritual, and cultural practices and teachings of the Jewish people handed down, mainly by oral tradition, from generation to generation. Folklore might include popular tales, legends, songs, and anecdotes that are transmitted primarily by word of mouth.

Finally, a superstition is any custom or act that is based on an irrational fear rather than on tradition, belief, reason, or knowledge.

What is midrash?

Midrash is the process by which Jews in every generation have grappled with the underlying significance of biblical texts. It contains homiletical interpretation of the Bible, sermonic teachings, ethical maxims, popular sayings and legends. The best-known is the *Midrash Rabbah* ("Great Midrash"), consisting of ten books of homiletic interpretations of the Five Books of Moses and the Five Megillot.

What are responsa?

Responsa are written replies given to questions about all aspects of Jewish law by qualified authorities from the talmudic period to the present. The questions asked by the individuals of their rabbis were often based on some current situation which was not directly dealt with in the codes. For example, is it permissible to use a life sustaining device to keep a patient alive? The rabbi would give his responsum (answer), basing his reasoning on support statements and earlier precedents found in the Bible, the Talmud and, later, the *Shulchan Aruch.* In this way Jewish law continued to develop, change, and be modified in order to be in consonance with new times and new situations.

What is the Rabbinical Assembly Committee on Jewish Law and Standards?

The Rabbinical Assembly is the professional organization for all Conservative rabbis. The Committee on Jewish Law and Standards, whose task it is to interpret Jewish law for the Conservative movement, consists of twenty-five rabbis appointed by the President of the Rabbinical Assembly. Its decisions were formerly issued as reflecting a majority and minority opinion. Nowadays, acceptance by six members of a position paper under discussion constitutes a legitimate opinion and official position. However, only when the opinion is unanimous and has been raised to the level of a standard of rabbinic practice by a convention of the Rabbinical Assembly is it incumbent upon the local rabbi to follow the decision of the Committee of Law and Standards.

The committee has rendered numerous decisions over the years which have impacted upon Conservative Judaism and the way in which it is observed. Among these decisions are the clarification of the use of electricity on *Shabbat,* the permission to use an automobile to drive to and from the synagogue on *Shabbat,* the inclusion of women in the minyan, the extension to women of the right to serve as rabbis and cantors, and the attempt to solve the problem of a woman whose husband refuses to grant her a Jewish divorce (get).

Is there one code of Jewish law for Conservative Jews?

There is no standard code of Jewish law that all Conservative Jews are expected to follow. However, one of the most important codes of Jewish law to be produced by the Conservative movement was published in 1979 (an augmented edition was published in 1992). Written by Rabbi Isaac Klein, a leading authority on Jewish law, the volume is entitled *A Guide to Jewish Religious Practice*. This guide was compiled and written in the spirit of the Conservative movement. It presents both the so-called normative Jewish practice and the decisions reached by the Rabbinical Assembly Committee on Law and Standards. It deals with such contemporary issues as artificial insemination, organ transplants, and autopsies, reflecting some of the most recent scientific advances of our day, and the burial of cremated remains in a Jewish cemetery.

2

Jewish Parenting Ceremony

It is good to give thanks to God. . .

—Psalm 136

*T*he Conservative movement has always sought continuity with tradition as well as relevance to the world of the present. The following ceremony marks new parenthood.

What is a Jewish Parenting Ceremony?

In the past two decades there has been a renewed interest in reinterpreting Jewish rituals and experimenting with new ones to celebrate special moments in one's Jewish life. A woman's pregnancy has given rise to special ceremonies to be observed prior to the birth of the baby and which are meant to facilitate the woman's transition into motherhood. Each ceremony generally contained its own uniquely developed theme reflecting the Jewish mother-to-be's feelings about the meaning of her pregnancy and thoughts about becoming a mother.

Are there any guidelines for planning and creating a prebirth ceremony?

The following suggested guidelines are courtesy of Shoshana Zonderman, whose own personal experiences and unique ceremony appeared in an article in *Response Magazine* (Spring 1985) entitled "Spiritual Preparation for Parenthood."

1. When planning any ceremony, pick an overall theme or image that reflects your own feelings about the pregnancy. Zonderman chose the image of a difficult passage through a tunnel ending in emergence as a mother. This image paralleled the Exodus of the Jews from Egypt. Following their escape from the tunnel of Egyptian oppression—a birth process with the water imagery of the parting of the Red Sea—the Israelites accepted a covenant at Mount Sinai with a host of new

responsibilities. Similarly, in becoming a parent, one must accept new responsibilities and a commitment to the future of the Jewish people.

2. Next, one must choose a suitable date for the ceremony to take place. Zonderman chose the evening of *Rosh Chodesh* (the New Moon) in the last month of her pregnancy. The New Moon has come to be viewed as a women's festival, since, according to legend, women refused to contribute their jewelry to construct the Golden Calf. Their reward was the celebration of the New Moon festival. Eleven women were invited to the ceremony, making a total of twelve women. This was a reminder of both the twelve tribes of Israel and the twelve lunar months of the Hebrew calendar.

3. Next, one must decide on the specific items/objects to be included in the ceremony. Zonderman chose five objects that represented her Jewish commitment and identity as a woman. The first and second items were a crescent-shaped *challah* and a pair of white, egg-shaped candles. The third item was a bowl of water, symbolizing the theme of birth.

   To expand the sensory aspect of the ritual, the fourth object was incense made from cedarwood. (Cedar, you may remember, was used in the Jerusalem tabernacle.) Lastly, a Kiddush cup with sweet red wine added to the festive occasion.

4. Each of the eleven women was asked to bring an egg-shaped candle and a fruit, symbolic of her wish for the mother-to- be.

5. The ceremony began with the lighting of a candle and the reciting by Zonderman of her Hebrew name and

matrilineage. Each of the other women in turn lit her candle and repeated the process. Next, the *shehecheeyanu*, the prayer for the gift of life, was recited by the women, followed by a series of movement and breathing exercises that took the women through the unfolding stages of a blooming bud.

6. Next, the blessings over the wine and bread were recited, after which each woman spoke and offered her personal wish that was presented by a fruit.

7. The ceremony concluded with some words from the mother-to-be describing her feelings during pregnancy. This was followed by the singing of some Psalms (including Psalms 130 and 136) and some spontaneous sharing of personal birthing experiences by the eleven women. The very end of the ceremony was spent reciting the Hebrew blessing for eating fruit and then tasting each of the fruits.

3

Brit Milah

He that is eight days old shall be circumcised ...
—Gen. 17:12

SOME HISTORICAL BACKGROUND

What is the meaning of Brit Milah?

The word *Brit* is a Hebrew word meaning "covenant" or "agreement." The word *Milah* is Hebrew for "circumcision." The Torah describes three major covenants. In the early part of the Book of Genesis, God made a covenant with Noah after the rains stopped, promising that He would never again destroy the entire world with a flood. The sign of this first covenant was a rainbow in the sky (Genesis 9:9–17). In another covenant described in the Book of Exodus, God made a pact with Israel through Moses. So long as His people would keep the commandments, God would protect them. The signs of this covenant were the Ten Commandments and the Sabbath (Exodus 24 and Exodus 31:18). Another covenant is mentioned in chapter 17 of the Book of Genesis, when God said to Abraham: "Every male among you shall be circumcised. You shall circumcise the flesh of your foreskin, and that shall be the sign of the covenant between you and Me. At the age of eight days, every male shall be circumcised." According to the Bible, Abraham followed God's command and not only circumcised his male children but even circumcised himself at age ninety-nine! The circumcision became a symbol for Abraham and his male descendants that they would observe God's ways and obey His commandments. Just as Abraham made this agreement, so the Jewish people, by means of this ceremony of circumcision, accept this covenant from generation to generation. Circumcision is Judaism's first rite of passage for boys, performed with prayers and prescribed rules and regulations as a religious spiritual act, not merely as a surgical procedure.

Did the Brit Milah ceremony originate with the Jews?

The practice of circumcising male children is as old as recorded history. The ancient Egyptians and Sumerians practiced circumcision. In more recent times, circumcision was practiced by the Aztecs, the Peruvians, and some of the peoples of Africa, Indonesia, and the Philippines. Some Eskimos and American Indians also circumcise as a rite of tribal initiation into manhood.

Among other peoples, circumcision can take place either at birth or as late as adolescence just prior to marriage. Only Judaism requires circumcision on the eighth day. And Judaism has given this first rite of passage true religious and national significance.

How important has circumcision been to Jewish survival?

Throughout Jewish history the act of circumcision has held a powerful religious influence upon the Jewish people. In biblical times, the failure to circumcise one's male child on the eighth day was punishable by excommunication from the Israelite community. The Bible relates that God was even ready to kill Moses for not circumcising his son Gershom (Exodus 4:24). The prophet Ezekiel emphasized the importance of *Brit Milah* to Jewish survival, pointing out to the Jewish people that the Babylonians and Assyrians among whom the Jews lived did not practice circumcision (Ezekiel 44:9).

The first major crisis in connection with the Brit Milah occurred during the reign of King Antiochus in the Book of the Maccabees. Although the king prohibited the Jews from circumcising their children, they persisted, even at the risk of losing their lives.

The Roman Emperor Hadrian also prohibited the *Brit Milah* in the early part of the first century. The Jewish people continued their observance of this important rite of passage, sometimes knowing full well that death was the penalty if they were caught.

Brit Milah has thus survived every challenge put to it, including a major one from anticircumcision movements in the world today. Nevertheless *Brit Milah* continues to be a powerful Jewish rite of passage that is observed in every major stream of Judaism throughout the world.

BRIT MILAH: PREPARATION

Now that we have reviewed some background related to the *Brit Milah,* we are ready to examine the preparation necessary to properly carry out the ceremony.

Who performs at a Brit Milah?

Traditionally, it is the basic duty of every Jewish father to circumcise his son. Abraham, you will remember, circumcised both Ishmael and Isaac. Since few fathers are able to do this with competency, it has become customary to appoint a *mohel* ("ritual circumciser") to do this for them. A *mohel* is a Jew who is specially trained in the surgical procedures and Jewish customs and traditions related to the *Brit Milah* ceremony. According to Jewish law both males and females may serve as ritual circumcisers (*mohalim/mohalot*). It often happens in smaller Jewish communities that no qualified *mohel* is available. In such cases a Jewish physician who knows the correct procedure and the prayers may be asked to perform the *Brit.* It is also customary to invite a rabbi to supervise the procedure and to assist in conducting the service.

Recently the Jewish Theological Seminary of America has been conducting a *Brit Kodesh* course in ritual circumcision for Jewish physicians. Both male and female doctors who are observant are encouraged to participate in the program. This will help to ensure that there will always be an adequate number of *mohalim* and *mohalot* in Jewish communities throughout the country.

When and where does the Brit Milah take place?

The ceremony of *Brit Milah* is celebrated on the eighth day after birth, even if that day falls on *Shabbat* or a Jewish holiday. Mornings are preferable so as to show zeal in the performance of the *Brit Milah*, which is a *mitzvah* ("religious commandment"). Thus if a child is born on a Monday during the day, the *Brit Milah* ceremony should take place on Monday morning. If a child is ill and the physician advises a postponement, the circumcision is postponed for as long as the physician deems necessary.

The *Brit Milah* ceremony may be held in the synagogue, the hospital, or the home. Today the home seems to be the first choice, since its environment is warm and most conducive to a family gathering.

Who should come to the Brit Milah ceremony?

Since the *Brit Milah* ceremony is a way of initiating a Jewish child into the House of Israel, it is appropriate to notify the entire community. Relatives, family and friends all enjoy sharing in the happiness of such an occasion. If possible, there should be a *minyan* (ten adult Jewish persons) at the *Brit Milah*, although this is not essential.

Who are the participants during the Brit Milah Ceremony and what do they do?

In addition to the mohel or a Jewish physician and the

rabbi, the following are the other participants in the actual *Brit Milah* ceremony:

Kvater: This is a German-derived word which means godfather. His ritual role is to bring the child into the room for the circumcision.

Kvaterin: This is a German-derived word which means godmother. Along with the *kvater,* the *kvaterin* also brings the child into the room where the circumcision will be performed. The *kvater* and *kvaterin* are often grandparents of the newborn, although aunts, uncles, cousins and friends may also be used.

Sandek: This is a Greek term meaning "with child." The *sandek*'s role is to hold the baby while the *mohel or mohelet* or a Jewish physician performs the surgical procedure of circumcision.

Elijah the Prophet: Jewish legend holds that Elijah the Prophet is present at every *Brit Milah* ceremony. This is because Elijah complained bitterly (I Kings 19:10–14) that the Jews would become assimilated since they have forsaken the observance of *Brit Milah.* Often considered today as the angel of the covenant, a special chair called the *kisay shel Eliyahu* (the "chair of Elijah") is used in Elijah's honor. The baby is placed upon the chair prior to the surgery. This symbolically enables Elijah to be present in spirit at every *Brit Milah.*

What sort of meal should we plan after the Brit Milah ceremony?

The festive meal following the *Brit Milah* is called a *seudat mitzvah,* a religious meal celebrating the observance of a Jewish commandment. This feast is considered an integral part of the religious event and therefore it is most appropriate that it conform to the Jewish dietary laws of *Kashrut* and include *Hamotzi* (the blessing over the bread) and *Birkat HaMazon* (the blessings after the meal).

What is a Shalom Zachar?

Shalom Zachar is the ceremony for "welcoming the son." It can also mean "peace of the male child" and is derived from a talmudic phrase which states that "peace comes when a male child is born" (Niddah 31b). The *Shalom Zachar* ceremony is usually celebrated on the Friday evening prior to the *Brit Milah* ceremony, either in the synagogue or in the home. As neighbors and friends gather in the home of the newborn, the rabbi often speaks some words of Torah in honor of the occasion and offers his blessing to the child. This is followed by the serving of refreshments. In some places lentils and chickpeas are served. They are round in shape and have come to symbolize life's continuity.

When a girl is born there are some families that will hold a *Shalom Nekevah* ceremony that parallels the ceremony of the *Shalom Zachar* previously described. The *Shalom Zachar* ceremony is less popular today in Conservative Judaism than it was in the past. There are, however, still comunities of Conservative Jews that have continued practicing this ceremony.

Are there any other customs that commemorate the arrival of a baby?

There are several lesser-known Jewish customs that are often linked to the *Brit Milah* ceremony. Traditionally, Jews mark happy occasions with contributions of *tzedakah,* righteous giving. This is a way of sharing the happiness of the occasion with others who are less fortunate. Some people will make a charitable donation to honor the birth of a child. Among Ashkenazic Jews it is common to give some multiple of eighteen dollars because the number value for eighteen is spelled out with the Hebrew letters for the word life—*chai*. Among Sephardic Jews, the number twenty-six, the number equivalent of God's name, is the basis for giving.

The idea of "twinning," linking a lifecycle event between an American Jew and a Soviet refusenik or an Ethiopian Jew, is most often associated with bar and bat mitzvah ceremonies. However, there are some families that choose to bring this custom to their *Brit Milah* ceremony. By speaking the name of a Soviet or Ethiopian child (or any child in a country where a family cannot freely practice its Judaism), American Jews affirm their solidarity with them. Any local Jewish agency will be able to assist you to find appropriate persons with whom to twin.

BRIT MILAH: THE CEREMONY

What is the order of the traditional service?

There is a custom to place two candles in the room where the ceremony is to take place, as a symbol of God's light and Presence.

1. The *kvater* (godfather) and *kvaterin* (godmother) bring the baby into the room. All present stand and say *Baruch ha-bah*, which means "Blessed be he who comes."
2. Next the father will frequently be asked by the *mohel* or *mohelet* to officially designate him or her as the one who will perform the circumcision.
3. The baby is placed on the table or on the lap of the *sandek*, and the rabbi, the *mohel* or another officiant

will generally briefly explain the significance of the ceremony.

4. The *sandek* will hold the baby and the officiant will then say this blessing:

בָּרוּךְ אַתָּה יְיָ אֱלֹהֵינוּ מֶלֶךְ הָעוֹלָם, אֲשֶׁר קִדְּשָׁנוּ בְּמִצְוֹתָיו וְצִוָּנוּ עַל הַמִּילָה.

Baruch ata Adonai elohenu melech haolam asher kid-shanu bemitzvotav vetzivanu al hamilah.

Praised are You God, Ruler of the Universe who has made us holy through Your *mitzvot* and commanded us concerning circumcision.

The circumcision is then performed. The actual operation consists of the following three steps:

• *Milah,* the cutting off of the foreskin.
• *Periah,* the tearing off and folding back of the mucous membrance to expose the glans. (The use of a clamp today by the mohel has made *milah* and *periah* one process.)
• *Metzitzah,* the suction of the blood from the wound, in order to prevent infection.

5. After the circumcision is completed, the father, and quite often the mother too, recites the following blessing:

בָּרוּךְ אַתָּה יְיָ אֱלֹהֵינוּ מֶלֶךְ הָעוֹלָם, אֲשֶׁר קִדְּשָׁנוּ בְּמִצְוֹתָיו וְצִוָּנוּ לְהַכְנִיסוֹ בִּבְרִיתוֹ שֶׁל אַבְרָהָם אָבִינוּ.

Baruch ata Adonai elohenu melech haolam asher kid-shanu bemitzvotav vetzivanu lehachniso bevrito shel Avra-ham Avinu.

Blessed are You, God, Sovereign of the Universe who has made us holy through Your *mitzvot* and

commanded us to bring our son into the covenant of
Abraham our ancestor.

6. All of those present then respond:

כְּשֵׁם שֶׁנִּכְנַס לַבְּרִית כֵּן יִכָּנֵס לְתוֹרָה וּלְחֻפָּה וּלְמַעֲשִׂים טוֹבִים:

*Keshem shenichnas levrit ken yikanes leTorah, ulechuppah
ulemaasim tovim.*

As he has entered the covenant, so too may he enter
a life of Torah, marriage, and good deeds.

7. The officiant then recites a blessing over a cup of wine,
which includes the formal naming of the baby. The
derivation of the baby's name will often be explained
prior to the formal naming. This is often done by parents
of the child, and can be a very moving and spiritual
experience, especially if the baby is being named for a
relative who has died.

בָּרוּךְ אַתָּה יְיָ אֱלֹהֵינוּ מֶלֶךְ הָעוֹלָם, בּוֹרֵא פְּרִי הַגָּפֶן.
בָּרוּךְ אַתָּה יְיָ אֱלֹהֵינוּ מֶלֶךְ הָעוֹלָם, אֲשֶׁר קִדַּשׁ יְדִיד מִבֶּטֶן,
וְחֹק בִּשְׁאֵרוֹ שָׂם וְצֶאֱצָאָיו חָתַם בְּאוֹת בְּרִית קוֹדֶשׁ. עַל כֵּן
בִּשְׂכַר זֹאת, אֵל חַי חֶלְקֵנוּ צוּרֵנוּ, צַוֵּה לְהַצִּיל יְדִידוּת שְׁאֵרֵנוּ
מִשַּׁחַת, לְמַעַן בְּרִיתוֹ אֲשֶׁר שָׂם בִּבְשָׂרֵנוּ. בָּרוּךְ אַתָּה יְיָ, כּוֹרֵת
הַבְּרִית.
אֱלֹהֵינוּ וֵאלֹהֵי אֲבוֹתֵינוּ, קַיֵּם אֶת־הַיֶּלֶד הַזֶּה לְאָבִיו וּלְאִמּוֹ,
וְיִקָּרֵא שְׁמוֹ בְּיִשְׂרָאֵל ____ בֶּן ____. יִשְׂמַח הָאָב בְּיוֹצֵא חֲלָצָיו
וְתָגֵל אִמּוֹ בִּפְרִי בִטְנָהּ, כַּכָּתוּב: יִשְׂמַח אָבִיךְ וְאִמֶּךְ וְתָגֵל
יוֹלַדְתֶּךָ. וְנֶאֱמַר: וָאֶעֱבוֹר עָלַיִךְ וָאֶרְאֵךְ מִתְבּוֹסֶסֶת בְּדָמָיִךְ
וָאֹמַר לָךְ בְּדָמַיִךְ חֲיִי, וָאֹמַר לָךְ בְּדָמַיִךְ חֲיִי. וְנֶאֱמַר: זָכַר
לְעוֹלָם בְּרִיתוֹ, דָּבָר צִוָּה לְאֶלֶף דּוֹר. אֲשֶׁר כָּרַת אֶת־אַבְרָהָם
וּשְׁבוּעָתוֹ לְיִצְחָק. וַיַּעֲמִידֶהָ לְיַעֲקֹב לְחֹק לְיִשְׂרָאֵל בְּרִית עוֹלָם.

וְנֶאֱמַר: וַיָּמָל אַבְרָהָם אֶת־יִצְחָק בְּנוֹ בֶּן שְׁמוֹנַת יָמִים, כַּאֲשֶׁר צִוָּה אֹתוֹ אֱלֹהִים. הוֹדוּ לַיְיָ כִּי טוֹב, כִּי לְעוֹלָם חַסְדּוֹ. זֶה הַקָּטֹן _____ גָּדוֹל יִהְיֶה. כְּשֵׁם שֶׁנִּכְנַס לַבְּרִית כֵּן יִכָּנֵס לְתוֹרָה וּלְחֻפָּה וּלְמַעֲשִׂים טוֹבִים. אָמֵן.

Praised are You, Adonai, Sovereign of the Universe, who has created the fruit of the vine.

Praised are You, Adonai, Sovereign of the Universe, who has sanctified the well-beloved (Isaac) from the womb and has set Your statute in his flesh, and has sealed his offspring with the sign of Your holy covenant. Therefore, God, deliver from destruction the dearly beloved of our flesh, for the sake of the covenant You have set in our bodies. Praised are You, Adonai, who has made the covenant.

Our God and God of our ancestors, preserve this child to his father and mother, and let his name be called in Israel _____, the son of _____[father] and _____[mother]. Let them rejoice in their offspring, as it is written: "Let your father and mother rejoice, and let her that bore you be glad." And it is said: "And I passed by you, and I saw you wallowing in your blood, and I said to you: 'In your blood shall you live.' I said: 'In your blood you shall live.' [There is a custom of putting some wine in the mouth of the baby when the last two sentences are repeated.] And it is said: God has remembered the covenant forever, the word which God commanded to a thousand generations, the covenant with Abraham, Isaac, and Jacob. And it is said: "Abraham circumcised his son Isaac when he was eight days old, as God commanded him." Give thanks to God, for God is good and God's kindness lasts forever. May this child _____ grow into adulthood as a blessing to his

family, the Jewish people and humankind. As he has
entered the covenant, so may he attain the blessings
of Torah, marriage, and a life of good deeds. Amen.

8. The baby is now blessed by the officiant:

יְבָרֶכְךָ יְיָ וְיִשְׁמְרֶךָ,

יָאֵר יְיָ פָּנָיו אֵלֶיךָ וִיחֻנֶּךָּ,

יִשָּׂא יְיָ פָּנָיו אֵלֶיךָ וְיָשֵׂם לְךָ שָׁלוֹם.

May God bless you and watch you,
May God's Presence shine His spirit on you and be
good to you,
May God grant you a blessing of peace.
Amen.

Are there any new customs related to Brit Milah?

Recently, there has been renewed interest in looking for
ways to honor family and friends during the *Brit Milah* ceremony. Sometimes, the baby is passed from one generation to
the next, from the grandparents (or great-grandparents) to
the parents. An older sibling might be honored by carrying
the baby into the room or offering a blessing.

Before the circumcision some parents will say a few words
about the baby's name. If he is being named for a deceased
relative, this can be a very touching and moving moment.
Sometimes a family member will also give a *devar Torah*
(Bible lesson) relating the Torah portion of the week to
some wishes for the baby and his future life.

Finally, some parents provide a printed guide that explains
the history and the meaning of *Brit Milah,* or provides
responsive readings and an explanation of the baby's Hebrew
name. The pamphlet might also include the prayers recited
after the meal.

SPECIAL CIRCUMSTANCES

What is a symbolic circumcision, or hatafat dam brit?

Jewish law indicates specifically that a *Brit Milah* ceremony must take place on the eighth day, unless there are medical problems related to the baby's health. The eighth day is determined by starting with the day of birth as the first day; the *Brit* therefore usually takes place on the same day of the week on which the baby was born.

If perchance a baby is medically circumcised but the proper blessings are not recited or the circumcision did not take place on the prescribed eighth day, then a symbolic circumcision, known as a *hatafat dam brit* (spilling of a drop of blood) takes place. This ceremony which involves a pinprick that lets out a spot of blood, must be done by a *mohel* or *mohelet* or by a qualified physician. The *hatafat dam brit* ceremony is also used for a non–Jewish adult male (who has been surgically circumcised) who converts to Judaism. Also non-Jewish children who convert to Judaism and who have been previously surgically circumcised without the ritual blessings require a *hatafat dam brit* according to Jewish law.

ARE THERE OTHER FOLK CUSTOMS RELATED TO BRIT MILAH?

Folk customs and superstitions surrounding the birth of children are found in every culture. Judaism, too, has its share of folk customs related to the birth of a child.

1. Placing red ribbons and garlic on a baby's crib to ward off evil spirits.
2. Placing a knife under the pillow of the mother the night before the *Brit Milah* to protect her from evil spirits.

3. During a difficult labor, place a Torah belt around the belly of the mother.

4. Placing candy under the bed of the new mother to draw the attention of evil spirits away from her and the baby.

5. In Israel there is a custom of planting a tree in honor of the new baby. When the child is grown the branches of the tree are then used as the poles for the wedding canopy (*chuppah*).

6. In Western Europe a custom arose of using the linen wrapping worn by the baby into an embroidered Torah binder. On the binder, called a "wimpel," the embroidered name of the baby, his date of birth and astrological sign was sewn. The wimpel was presented to the congregation on the occasion of the baby's first birthday.

7. During the period of the Middle Ages there arose a custom of "cradling" the baby boy after his circumcision. In this ceremony a copy of the Five Books of Moses was placed upon him in his cradle, and the people standing about him said, "May this child fulfill what is written in this book!" Unfortunately today this practice has been discontinued, although it may be a nice way to inspire learning again in the Jewish community.

8. In Eastern Europe it was customary to throw sugar, raisins, cake, and coins into the baby's cradle before the child was placed in it, as an omen for a sweet and abundant life.

WHAT ARE THE JEWISH OBLIGATIONS OF PARENTS AND CHILDREN TO EACH OTHER?

The importance of the family is paramount to Judaism. The very origin of the nation of Israel is traced to one family and it is therefore no wonder that the family is considered the very cornerstone of the Jewish social fabric. Exceptional emphasis is laid in Judaism upon children honoring parents and vice versa. Throughout the ages the rabbis have written and spoken about various aspects of the Jewish family. The following is a selection of these writings and statements throughout the ages.

Family and Home

1. A home where Torah is not heard will not endure. (Intr. Tikkune Zohar 6a)
2. Anger in a home is like a worm in a fruit. (Sotah 3b)
3. A man should honor his wife and children with even more than he can afford. (Hullin 84b)
4. A woman of valor, who can find, for her worth is far above rubies. (Proverbs 31:10)

Children

1. Do not threaten a child. Either punish or forgive him. (Semachot 2:6)
2. He who denies a child religious knowledge robs him of his inheritance. (Sanhedrin 91b)
3. One who hits a child violates the biblical precept: You shall not place a stumbling block before the blind. (Leviticus 19:14)
4. Mothers should introduce their children to the Torah. (Exodus Rabbah 28:2)
5. The proverb runs: He who is descended from you often teaches you. (Pesikta Zutarta, Bereshit 26)
6. When a child honors his father and mother, the Holy One, Blessed be He, says: "I consider it as though I were being honored." (Niddah 31a)
7. Every parent is obligated to train his children in the observance of *mitzvot*, for it is written: "Train a child according to his way." (Proverbs 22:6)

Parents

1. The honor due to parents is like the honor due to God. (Judah HaNasi, Mekhilta, to Exodus 20:12)
2. To honor parents is more important even than to honor God. (Simeon B. Yochai, Y. Peah 1:1.)
3. Whether you have wealth or not, honor your parents. (Y. Peah 1:1)
4. A man honors his mother more than his father; therefore, God has placed the father first in the commandment to honor. A man fears his father more than his mother; therefore, the mother is placed first in the commandment to fear. (Kiddushin, 30b–31a)
5. Engaging in the study of Torah and good deeds is the greatest way to bestow honor on parents. (Talmud)

4

What Shall We Name Our Child?

A fair name is better than precious oil.
                                        —Ecclesiastes 7:1

*B*ACKGROUND

Is naming a child important in Judaism?

The Bible portrays naming as one of the first independent human acts. Adam's job in the Garden of Eden (Genesis 2:20) was to give names to the animals and birds! The Bible also emphasizes the importance of names in its description of several dramatic instances of name changes. For instance, once Abram and Sarai accept God's covenant, their names are changed to Abraham and Sarah. Perhaps the most dramatic name change was that of Jacob, who, after wrestling with the angel, is given the name Israel, meaning champion of God (Genesis 32:29).

Several biblical personalities were named after plants and animals. Tamar means a palm tree, Jonah means a dove, and Deborah means a bee. Biblical children were rarely, if ever, named after relatives, either living or dead. None of the twenty-one kings of Judea, for example, were named after a predecessor.

When did Jews begin naming children after other people?

The custom of naming children after other persons began in the sixth century B.C.E. Since there were no laws concerning the naming of children, much of what the Jews did then and much of what Jews observe today in this area is custom and is sometimes based on folklore or superstition. Ashkenazic Jews customarily chose to memorialize a deceased relative by bestowing that person's name upon a newborn child. However, they did not use the names of a living relative, because of the belief that a person's name carries with it both the power and characteristics of that person. Naming a child for a living person would, therefore, they believed, reduce the power and shorten the life of that relative. Similarly, they would often choose not to name a child for a deceased relative who had died early in life, lest a similar fate await the newborn. On the other hand, Sephardic Jews would often name babies after the living, usually a parent or grandparent. To the Sephardim this custom was an expression of honoring the living! Today, these two naming patterns continue as customs in Ashkenazic and Sephardic communities throughout the world.

When are Jewish boys and girls given their Hebrew names?

As previously noted, a boy receives his Hebrew name on the eighth day after birth at the ceremony of his *Brit Milah.* A girl is customarily named in the synagogue on a day when the Torah is read, although it is technically permissible for a girl to be named in her family's home or on a day when the Torah is not read. There is no prescribed time for naming a Jewish girl, but it is recommended that it be done as soon as possible after her birth, since one always hastens to perform a *mitzvah*!

What are some Jewish teachings related to names?

There are many interesting statements in Judaism related to the importance of a good and respected name. Here are several for your consideration:

1. A good name is better than fine oil. (Ecclesiastes 7:1)
2. A good name is preferable to wealth. (Proverbs 22:1)
3. Every person has three names: one parents give them, one others call them, and one they acquire themselves." (Ecclesiastes Rabbah)
4. There are three crowns, the crown of Torah, the crown of royalty, and the crown of priesthood, but the crown

of a good name excels them all." (Ethics of Our Fathers
   4:13)
5. The name of a person can determine his destiny. (Berachot
   7b)

*What folklore and superstitions surround the naming of Jewish
children?*

Throughout Jewish history, names have been said to hold
special power. It is therefore not surprising that a number
of superstitions and folklore developed. Here are several for
you to think about:

1. In early times it was the custom to name a child immediately upon birth. Later the naming was postponed
   because it was feared that the name presented a "handle"
   with which the baby could be reached by the Angel of
   Death. It was thought that by postponing the naming
   the Angel of Death could not reach the child during the
   most fragile first days of life.
2. In the Middle Ages some Jews had secret names that they
   would not reveal to anyone.
3. Some Jews follow a custom of refusing to marry a person
   who has the same name as their mother or father. This
   custom arises from fear that the Angel of Death might
   confuse two persons with the same name, leading to the
   premature death of one or the other.
4. In Eastern Europe children would sometimes be given
   additional names that symbolized length of years, such
   as the Yiddish name "Alter," meaning old person. Giving
   a child such a name was believed to increase one's
   longevity.
5. A custom that is still seen today was to change the
   name of a person who was extremely ill and near death.
   Accordingly, such a person might be given the new name

of Chayim ("life" for a male) or Chaya ("living being" for a female) in order to deceive the angel of a death through this change in identity.

Where can I look for some biblical or modern Hebrew names?

The task of choosing a Hebrew name can be a wonderful experience. Since Jewish names have several sources, you have a number of possibilities. Your first source of information is the Bible. There are almost three thousand biblical names from which you can choose! You may want to consult one of the many Jewish name dictionaries (see Bibliography) which offer many possibilities. Since it has become a custom among American Jews to have a Hebrew name along with a civil name, you may wish to bridge the gap between the two by providing an English name with an exact Hebrew equivalent. Examples in this category would include David, Miriam, Michal, and Leora.

What are the times when we use our Hebrew names?

Our Hebrew names will often be used by our religious teachers. They will also be used and needed when we are called to the Torah and during Jewish life cycle events. For example, every bar and bat mitzvah is customarily called to the Torah using a Hebrew name. The Hebrew names are also used on the *ketubah* (Jewish marriage contract) and on the *get* (Jewish divorce certificate). One's Hebrew name will be used in the series of *mi shebayrach* prayers, which includes prayers of blessing and prayers for a speedy recovery in the event of an illness. With relationship to death, it will also be used to chant final prayers at a funeral and quite often will be written on a gravestone.

What are the special components of the naming ceremony for girls?

There are many new and innovative naming ceremonies that have been created for girls in recent years. These ceremonies go by many names: *Simchat Bat* (joy of the daughter), *Brit Hachayim* (covenant of life), *Brit Kedusha* (covenant of sanctification) and *Brit Sarah,* (covenant of Sarah).In a Sephardic ceremony called a *zeved habat* (celebration for the gift of a daughter), special songs, ululations of joy, dancing and a lavish feast often accompany the naming ceremony. Each ceremony that takes written form is passed along to other parents, who almost always revise and reshape it to fit their own particular needs. The following are some elements culled from a variety of ceremonies which you might wish to include if you decide to design your own ceremony:

1. The baby is carried into the room with the officiant saying the words *Brucha haba'a* "Blessed is she who enters."
2. This is often followed by lighting of candles because the mitzvah of lighting Shabbat and holiday candles is given to women. (Note: If the ceremony takes place on Shabbat or a Jewish festival, the candles should be lit at the proper candle-lighting time.) A suggested blessing after lighting the candles is the following:

בָּרוּךְ אַתָּה יְיָ אֱלֹהֵינוּ מֶלֶךְ הָעוֹלָם, אֲשֶׁר קִדְּשָׁנוּ בְּמִצְוֹתָיו וְצִוָּנוּ עַל קְדוּשׁ הַחַיִּים.

Baruch ata Adonai elohenu melech ha'olam asher kidshanu b'mitzvotav vitzivanu al kiddush hachayim.

Blessed are You, Adonai, by whose *mitzvot* we are made holy and who commands us to sanctify life.

3. Next, the Kiddush over a cup of wine may be chanted, since it begins virtually every Jewish celebration:

בָּרוּךְ אַתָּה יְיָ אֱלֹהֵינוּ מֶלֶךְ הָעוֹלָם, בּוֹרֵא פְּרִי הַגֶּפֶן.

Baruch ata Adonai elohenu melech ha'olam boray pri hagafen.

Blessed are You, Adonai, who creates the fruit of the vine.

4. This next part of the female naming ceremony is called the "covenantal" part. It is often introduced with a blessing such as the following:

בָּרוּךְ אַתָּה יְיָ אֱלֹהֵינוּ מֶלֶךְ הָעוֹלָם, אֲשֶׁר קִדֵּשׁ יְדִיד הַבֶּטֶן.
אֵל חַי חֶלְקֵנוּ צוּרֵנוּ, צַוֵּה לְהַצִּיל יְדִידוּת שְׁאֵרֵנוּ מִשַּׁחַת,
לְמַעַן בְּרִיתוֹ. בָּרוּךְ אַתָּה יְיָ כּוֹרֵת הַבְּרִית.
אֱלוֹהַּ כָּל הַבְּרִיאוֹת קַיֵּם אֶת-הַיַּלְדָה הַזֹּאת לְאָבִיהָ וּלְאִמָּהּ.

You have sanctified your beloved from the womb and established Your holy covenant throughout the generations. May devotion to the covenant continue to sustain us as a people. Praised are You Adonai who has established the covenant. Blessed by the Presence whose sanctity fills our lives, we give thanks for the covenant.

The participants may then respond:

כְּשֵׁם שֶׁנִּכְנֶסֶת לַבְּרִית כֵּן תִּכָּנְסִי לְתוֹרָה וּלְחֻפָּה וּלְמַעֲשִׂים טוֹבִים.

K'shem shenich-nesest labrit ken tikansi l'torah, ul'chuppah ulemaasim tovim.

As she has entered the covenant, so may she enter a life devoted to Torah, the marriage canopy and the accomplishment of good deeds.

5. This part of the ceremony is the actual naming. It is appropriate for the officiant to explain the meaning of the Hebrew name to the participants. The officiant may then continue with this naming formula:

אֱלֹהֵינוּ וֵאלֹהֵי אִמּוֹתֵינוּ, קַיֵּם אֶת־הַיַּלְדָּה הַזֹּאת לְאָבִיהָ
וּלְאִמָּהּ, וְיִקָּרֵא שְׁמָהּ בְּיִשְׂרָאֵל ____ יִשְׂמַח הָאָב בְּיוֹצֵאת
חֲלָצָיו, וְתָגֵל אִמָּהּ בִּפְרִי בִטְנָהּ.

Our God and God of our ancestors, sustain this child along with her mother and father. Let her name be called _____ [insert Hebrew name] in Israel. May the mother and father rejoice with their child, as it is written, "Let your parents be happy; let your mother thrill with joy."

6. The ceremony generally continues by having the officiant or parents recite the three fold priestly benediction:

יְשִׂמֵךְ אֱלֹהִים כְּשָׂרָה רִבְקָה רָחֵל וְלֵאָה:

Yiseemech Eloheem keSarah, Rivka, Rachel veLeah.

May God make you as Sarah, Rebecca, Rachel and Leah.

יְבָרֶכְךָ יְיָ וְיִשְׁמְרֶךָ,

Yevarechecha Adonai v'yishmerecha

May God bless you and keep you.

יָאֵר יְיָ פָּנָיו אֵלֶיךָ וִיחֻנֶּךָּ,

Ya'er Adonai Panav Eylecha Veechuneka

May God's Presence shine and be good to you.

יִשָּׂא יְיָ פָּנָיו אֵלֶיךָ וְיָשֵׂם לְךָ שָׁלוֹם.

Yisa Adonai Panav Eylecha Veyasem Lecha Shalom.

May God's face turn toward you and give you peace.

7. The ceremony may conclude with the recitation by the parents of the baby reciting the prayer for the gift of life, known as the *shehecheeyanu*:

בָּרוּךְ אַתָּה יְיָ אֱלֹהֵינוּ מֶלֶךְ הָעוֹלָם שֶׁהֶחֱיָנוּ וְקִיְּמָנוּ וְהִגִּיעָנוּ לַזְּמַן הַזֶּה:

Baruch ata Adonai elohenu melech ha'olam shehecheeyanu vekeemanu veheegeeyanu lazman hazeh.

Praised are You Adonai who has kept us alive and sustained us and enabled us to reach this happy day.

A rousing chorus of *siman tov* and *mazal tov* will often end the ceremony and signal the commencement of the *seudat mitzvah,* the religious party. This meal traditionally begins with the blessing over bread:

בָּרוּךְ אַתָּה יְיָ אֱלֹהֵינוּ מֶלֶךְ הָעוֹלָם, הַמּוֹצִיא לֶחֶם מִן הָאָרֶץ:

Baruch ata Adonai elohenu melech ha'olam hamotzi lechem min ha'aretz.

Blessed are You Adonai who brings forth bread from the earth.

The Blessing after the Meal (*Birkat Hamazon*) is an appropriate prayer with which to conclude the meal, thanking God, the ultimate Provider of the food.

בָּרוּךְ אַתָּה יְיָ, אֱלֹהֵינוּ מֶלֶךְ הָעוֹלָם, הַזָּן אֶת־הָעוֹלָם כֻּלּוֹ בְּטוּבוֹ בְּחֵן בְּחֶסֶד וּבְרַחֲמִים הוּא נוֹתֵן לֶחֶם לְכָל־בָּשָׂר כִּי לְעוֹלָם חַסְדּוֹ,

וּבְטוּבוֹ הַגָּדוֹל תָּמִיד לֹא חָסַר לָנוּ וְאַל יֶחְסַר־לָנוּ מָזוֹן לְעוֹלָם
וָעֶד, בַּעֲבוּר שְׁמוֹ הַגָּדוֹל, כִּי הוּא אֵל זָן וּמְפַרְנֵס לַכֹּל, וּמֵטִיב לַכֹּל,
וּמֵכִין מָזוֹן לְכָל־בְּרִיּוֹתָיו אֲשֶׁר בָּרָא. בָּרוּךְ אַתָּה יְיָ, הַזָּן אֶת־הַכֹּל.

Baruch ata Adonai elohenu melech ha-olam, hazan et ha-olam kulo b'tuvo b'chein b'chesed uv-rachamim, hu notein lechem l'chol basar, ki l'olam chasdo, uv-tuvo hagadol tamid lo chasar lanu v'al yechsar lanu mazon l'olam va-ed. Ba-avur sh'mo hagadol ki hu zan um-farneis lakol u-meitiv lakol, u-meichin mazon l'chol b'riyotav asher bara. Baruch ata Adonai, hazan et hakol.

Praised are You, Adonai, our God, Ruler of the universe, who sustains the whole world with kindness and compassion. You provide food for every creature, for Your love endures forever. Your great goodness has never failed us. Your great glory assures us nourishment. All life is Your creation and You are good to all, providing every creature with food and sustenance. Praised are You, God who sustains all life.

CHECKLIST FOR BRIT MILAH AND NAMING PLANS
(including *Simchat Bat*)

This list will help you to keep track of the organization for your *Brit Milah* and naming plans.

Date and time of Birth _____

Date and Time of *Brit Milah* _____

Date and Time of Naming Ceremony _____

Name of *Mohel/Mohelet* or Jewish physician _____

Officiating clergy_____

Hebrew/Jewish name for our child _____

We have notified all of our guests_____

We have selected for our twinning ceremony _____

We have selected our participants for the ceremony:

The *kvater* is _____

The *kvaterin* is _____

The *sandek* is_____

We have arranged for a *shalom zachar/nekevah* which will take

place at _____

We have arranged for the *seudat mitzvah*

Our participants at the *seudat mitzvah* will be _____ to

lead the *Hamotzi* over the bread and _____ to lead the

Blessing after the Meal.

5

Pidyon Haben

The Lord spoke to Moses saying: Consecrate to me every firstborn, man and beast, the first issue of every womb among the Israelites is Mine.

—Exodus 13:1–2

HISTORICAL BACKGROUND

What is pidyon haben?

The Jewish people, like most religious groups, had special rites and responsibilities for its firstborn. The firstborn of any species, man or beast, was offered to God. Whereas some ancient peoples offered their firstborn as a sacrifice to their gods, the Jews consecrated their firstborn, endowing them with leadership and special responsibilities.

The firstborn Israelite son received the birthright, which made him the head of the entire family clan and the owner of the family's material possessions. In the Bible we read that Abraham passed the mantle of leadership to Isaac, his firstborn son of his wife Sarah.

Firstborn sons also play a very important role in the story of the exodus of the Jews from Egypt. Since the time of the tenth plague when the Egyptian firstborn were slain and the Israelites were saved, the firstborn were to be consecrated to God. "For every firstborn among the Israelites ... is Mine ... I consecrated them to Myself at the time that I smote every firstborn in the land of Egypt" (Numbers 8:17).

The situation changed when the Jews started their wanderings in the desert after having worshiped the golden calf. When a tabernacle (i.e., the portable sanctuary that took the form of a tent) was built in the wilderness, the special duties of the firstborn were transferred to the Levites, a priestly tribe, possibly as a punishment for the firstborn males committing idolatry during the golden calf episode. The Bible then decreed that every father release his firstborn son from his special duties by redeeming him from a *Kohen.* Since that time we follow the custom of releasing the firstborn male child of his ancient obligation with a ceremony called a *pidyon haben,* meaning "redemption of the firstborn son."

50

Who requires a pidyon haben ceremony?

1. Jewish law requires that a *pidyon haben* be performed if the child is male and the first "issue" of the womb. If the child's father is a *Kohen* or a *Levite*, that child will automatically belong to the special caste of ministers called *Kohanim* and *Leviim* and need not have a *pidyon haben*. Also, if the mother of the child is the daughter of a *Kohen* or a *Levi*, the rite is not performed.

2. A male child born by Caesarean operation does not have to be redeemed, because Jewish law does not consider such a child as "issuing forth" from the womb.

3. A son born of a woman who previously had a miscarriage would not have a *pidyon haben*; nor would a son born to a woman who had a previous stillbirth.

4. If a man marries twice, the firstborn son of each wife must be redeemed!

Where and when does a pidyon haben take place?

1. The Bible states (Numbers 18:16) that a child from a month old shall be redeemed." From this statement the rabbis deduced that a *pidyon haben* takes place after the first month of life, or thirty days after birth. Since Jews have always found it desirable to observe a religious ordinance as soon as possible, the *pidyon haben* generally takes place on the thirty-first day after birth. If the thirty-first day falls on a Sabbath or Festival, the redemption is postponed to the following day, since it is not appropriate according to Jewish law to conduct a ceremony involving the transferring of money on a holy day. If the thirty-first day falls during *Chol HaMoed* (intermediate days) of Passover or Sukkot, the redemption need not be postponed.

2. Since it may sometimes be difficult to have the *pidyon haben* during the daytime on a weekday, especially when people work and the days are short, it is permissible to hold a *pidyon haben* at night.

3. The *pidyon haben* ceremony is generally held in one's home, and family and friends are usually invited to attend and partake of the religious collation following the ceremony. It would of course also be permissible to hold a *pidyon haben* in the synagogue.

What does one need in order to conduct the ceremony?

These are the things that are needed in order to properly conduct a *pidyon haben* ceremony: A cup of wine, a *challah* (part of the festive meal to follow), a *Kohen*, the firstborn male son and his parents, five shekels (silver dollars are often used today, or one can also purchase silver coins which are specially minted for the *pidyon haben* ceremony and which are often donated to charity after the ceremony) and the officiant (usually the rabbi or cantor or a knowledgeable Jewish layperson).

What is the order of the ceremony of pidyon haben?

1. The father hands his son to the *Kohen* and says the following:

זֶה בְּנִי בְכוֹרִי הוּא פֶּטֶר רֶחֶם לְאִמּוֹ, וְהַקָּדוֹשׁ בָּרוּךְ הוּא צִוָּה לִפְדּוֹתוֹ, שֶׁנֶּאֱמַר: וּפְדוּיָו מִבֶּן חֹדֶשׁ תִּפְדֶּה בְּעֶרְכְּךָ כֶּסֶף חֲמֵשֶׁת שְׁקָלִים בְּשֶׁקֶל הַקֹּדֶשׁ, עֶשְׂרִים גֵּרָה הוּא. וְנֶאֱמַר: קַדֶּשׁ־לִי כָל בְּכוֹר, פֶּטֶר כָּל־רֶחֶם בִּבְנֵי יִשְׂרָאֵל בָּאָדָם וּבַבְּהֵמָה, לִי הוּא.

This my firstborn is the firstborn of his mother, and God has given command to redeem him, as it is

written in the Torah: When he is one month old you
shall redeem him for five shekels. And it is written:
Sanctify unto Me every firstborn Israelite; he is Mine.

2. Next, the father places before the *Kohen* the five silver
shekels and the *Kohen* asks the following:

מַאי בָּעֵית טְפֵי, לִתֵּן בִּנְךָ בְּכוֹרְךָ שֶׁהוּא פֶּטֶר רֶחֶם לְאִמּוֹ, אוֹ
בָּעֵית לִפְדּוֹתוֹ בְּעַד חָמֵשׁ סְלָעִים, כִּדְמְחַיַּבְתְּ מִדְּאוֹרַיְתָא?

What is your preference—to give me your firstborn
son or to redeem him for five shekels, as you are
commanded to do in the Torah?

3. The father gives the five shekels to the *Kohen* and says:

חָפֵץ אֲנִי לִפְדּוֹת אֶת־בְּנִי, וְהֵילָךְ דְּמֵי פִּדְיוֹנוֹ כִּדְמְחַיַּבְתִּי
מִדְּאוֹרַיְתָא.

I want to redeem my son. Here is the equivalent of
five shekels, and thus I fulfil my obligation according
to the Torah.

4. The *Kohen* receives the redemption money, returns the
child to his father, whereupon the father recites:

בָּרוּךְ אַתָּה יְיָ אֱלֹהֵינוּ מֶלֶךְ הָעוֹלָם, אֲשֶׁר קִדְּשָׁנוּ בְּמִצְוֹתָיו
וְצִוָּנוּ עַל פִּדְיוֹן הַבֵּן.

*Baruch ata Adonai elohenu melech ha'olam asher kid-
shanu bemitzvotav vetzivanu al pidyon haben.*

Praised are You, God, who made us holy with Your
mitzvot and commanded us concerning the redemption of the firstborn.

5. Father and mother now join in saying the prayer for the gift of life:

בָּרוּךְ אַתָּה יְיָ אֱלֹהֵינוּ מֶלֶךְ הָעוֹלָם שֶׁהֶחֱיָנוּ וְקִיְּמָנוּ וְהִגִּיעָנוּ לַזְּמַן הַזֶּה:

Baruch ata Adonai elohenu melech ha'olam shehecheeyanu vekeemanu veheegeeyanu lazman hazeh.

Praise are You God who has kept us alive, sustained us and enabled us to reach this day.

6. The *Kohen* then holds the coins and says:

זֶה תַּחַת זֶה, זֶה חִלּוּף זֶה, זֶה מָחוּל עַל זֶה. וְיִכָּנֵס זֶה הַבֵּן לְחַיִּים, לְתוֹרָה וּלְיִרְאַת שָׁמָיִם. יְהִי רָצוֹן, שֶׁכְּשֵׁם שֶׁנִּכְנַס לַפִּדְיוֹן כֵּן יִכָּנֵס לְתוֹרָה וּלְחֻפָּה וּלְמַעֲשִׂים טוֹבִים. אָמֵן.

I accept the five shekels and hereby declare your son redeemed. May he be granted a complete and full life, live in devotion to the Torah and with reverence for God. As this child has attained redemption, so may it be God's will that he attain the blessings of Torah, marriage and a life of good deeds.

7. The Kohen concludes by placing his hands upon the head of the child and reciting the threefold priestly blessing:

יְשִׂמְךָ אֱלֹהִים כְּאֶפְרַיִם וְכִמְנַשֶּׁה.

Yiseemcha Eloheem k'Efraim V'CheeMenasseh

May God make you like Ephraim and Menasseh

יְבָרֶכְךָ יְיָ וְיִשְׁמְרֶךָ,

Yevarechecha Adonai v'yishmerecha,

May God bless you and keep you,

יָאֵר יְיָ פָּנָיו אֵלֶיךָ וִיחֻנֶּךָּ,

Ya'er Adonai Panav Eylecha Veechuneka,

May God's Presence shine and be good to you,

יִשָּׂא יְיָ פָּנָיו אֵלֶיךָ וְיָשֵׂם לְךָ שָׁלוֹם.

Yisa Adonai Panav Eylecha Vayesem Lecha Shalom.

May God's face turn toward you and give you peace.

8. A blessing is said over the wine and *challah,* and a festive meal is usually served to the invited guests.

Blessing over Wine:

בָּרוּךְ אַתָּה יְיָ אֱלֹהֵינוּ מֶלֶךְ הָעוֹלָם, בּוֹרֵא פְּרִי הַגֶּפֶן.

Baruch ata Adonai elohenu melech ha'Olam boray pri hagafen

Praised are You God who creates the fruit of the vine.

Blessing over Challah:

בָּרוּךְ אַתָּה יְיָ אֱלֹהֵינוּ מֶלֶךְ הָעוֹלָם, הַמּוֹצִיא לֶחֶם מִן הָאָרֶץ:

Baruch ata Adonai elohenu melech ha'Olam haMotzi lechem min ha'aretz.

Praised are You God who brings forth bread from the earth.

9. The Blessing after the Meal (*Birkat HaMazon*) is the prayer after the meal intended to thank God as the Provider of the food.

בָּרוּךְ אַתָּה יְיָ, אֱלֹהֵינוּ מֶלֶךְ הָעוֹלָם, הַזָּן אֶת־הָעוֹלָם כֻּלּוֹ בְּטוּבוֹ בְּחֵן בְּחֶסֶד וּבְרַחֲמִים הוּא נוֹתֵן לֶחֶם לְכָל־בָּשָׂר כִּי לְעוֹלָם חַסְדּוֹ, וּבְטוּבוֹ הַגָּדוֹל תָּמִיד לֹא חָסַר לָנוּ וְאַל יֶחְסַר־ לָנוּ מָזוֹן לְעוֹלָם וָעֶד, בַּעֲבוּר שְׁמוֹ הַגָּדוֹל, כִּי הוּא אֵל זָן וּמְפַרְנֵס לַכֹּל, וּמֵטִיב לַכֹּל, וּמֵכִין מָזוֹן לְכָל־בְּרִיּוֹתָיו אֲשֶׁר בָּרָא. בָּרוּךְ אַתָּה יְיָ, הַזָּן אֶת־הַכֹּל.

Baruch ata Adonai elohenu melech ha-olam, hazan et ha-olam kulo b'tuvo b'chein b'chesed uv-rachamim, hu notein lechem l'chol basar, ki l'olam chasdo, uv-tuvo hagadol tamid lo chasar lanu v'al yechsar lanu mazon l'olam va-ed. Ba-avur sh'mo hagadol ki hu zan um-farneis lakol u-meitiv lakol, u-meichin mazon l'chol b'riyotav asher bara. Baruch ata Adonai, hazan et hakol.

Praised are You, Adonai, our God, Ruler of the universe, who sustains the whole world with kindness and compassion. You provide food for every creature, for Your love endures forever. Your great goodness has never failed us. Your great glory assures us nourishment. All life is Your creation and You are good to all, providing every creature with food and sustenance. Praised are You, God who sustains all life.

Pidyon Habat

Is there a ceremony for the redemption of daughters?

In recent years, as we accord similar honors to both male and female children, there are families that have created a personalized ritual for their firstborn daughters. Called by various names, *pidyon habat* ("redemption of the firstborn daughter") or *kiddush peter rechem* ("sanctification of the one who opens the womb") or *seder kidushat chaye hamishpacha* ("ceremony of consecration to family life"), they generally share certain elements, including a dialogue between the officiant and the parents relating to the importance of consecrating firstborn children, an exchange of coins which are donated to charity in honor of the firstborn girl, the priestly blessing and the recitation of the *shehecheeyanu* prayer. Of course the ceremony also concludes with a festive meal, similar in nature to that previously described.

The following is a sample *pidyon habat* ceremony which you may wish to use or adapt for your own personal needs.

Parents: This is our daughter, our firstborn, who opens the womb of her mother. As it is written: Consecrate to Me all the firstborn, whatever is the first to open the womb among the people of Israel (Exodus 13:2).

Having been privileged to realize the fulfillment of life, may our sense for the reverence and holiness of life be heightened.

Beloved are people for they are created in God's image. It is by special Divine love that we are informed that people are created in the image of God. Beloved are Israel, for they were called the children of God.

The consecration of every firstborn also reminds us of the Exodus from Egypt. As it is written: And when your child will ask you, "What does this mean?" you will say, "By strength of hand God has redeemed us out of the house of bondage" (Exodus 13:14).

וְהָיָה כִּי יִשְׁאָלְךָ בִנְךָ מָחָר לֵאמֹר מַה זֹאת וְאָמַרְתָּ אֵלָיו בְּחֹזֶק יָד הוֹצִיאָנוּ יְיָ מִמִּצְרַיִם מִבֵּית עֲבָדִים.

The Egyptian exodus has taught us the value of having our freedom and liberty. May we work to achieve freedom for all people, as we begin to create a home where love, kindness and compassion will always be a part of our family.

Officiant now asks parents: Blessed with the sacred trust of new life, will you dedicate yourselves to the redeeming of life?

Parents: We want our daughter to inspire us to work for the freedom and redemption of all people. In honor of the birth of our daughter, ____[name] bat ____(father) and ___[mother], we pledge this gift of *tzedakah*. It will always be the symbol of her commitment to the Torah and her involvement with the mission of improving the world through deeds of kindness and generosity. Praised are You, Adonai, whose holiness fills our lives. We redeem our firstborn daughter and commit her and our family to a life of working for the redemption of others. Amen.

[Parents bless their daughter with the priestly blessing. This is followed by the recitation of the *shehecheeyanu*.]

Parents: Praised are You, God, who has kept us in life and sustained us and enabled us to reach this occasion.

CHECKLIST FOR PIDYON HABEN/HABAT

This list will help you to keep track of your plans for organizing a *pidyon haben/habat.*

Date and Time of *Pidyon Haben/Habat*_____

Name of officiating clergy _____

Name of *Kohen* _____

We have contacted all of our guests _____

We have obtained five silver shekels _____

We have arranged for the *seudat mitzvah*

The blessing over the wine will be recited by _____

The blessing over the bread will be said by _____

The Blessing after the Meal will be led by _____

6

Bar/Bat Mitzvah

At thirteen one is ready to fulfil commandments
—Ethics of Our Fathers 5:23

HISTORICAL BACKGROUND

What is the meaning of bar/bat mitzvah?

Bar and *bat mitzvah* literally mean "son" and "daughter of the Commandment." The term *bat mitzvah* is Hebrew, while *bar mitzvah,* historically a somewhat earlier ceremony, is Aramaic. The Aramaic word *bar* is the equivalent of the Hebrew *ben,* meaning "son."

What event does the bar and bat mitzvah commemorate in Jewish life?

Historically, the bar mitzvah and then later the bat mitzvah represented a Jewish rite of passage when a child reached the age when he or she was responsible for the performance of *mitzvot.* According to Jewish law, these new responsibilities occurred when a boy became age thirteen and a girl became age twelve.

What is the origin of the bar mitzvah?

It will certainly seem strange to many people that the origin of the bar mitzvah ceremony is shrouded in mystery and scholarly debate. The Bible neither mentions a bar mitzvah celebration nor gives any indication that thirteen was considered the demarcation line between the status of being a minor and an adult. In fact, when a particular age is mentioned in the Bible as a requirement or test for full participation in the community's activities, the age given is twenty, not thirteen. In Exodus (30:14), we read of a census that was taken among the Israelites. Only those twenty of age or older were to be counted in the census. In Leviticus (27:1–5), the valuation of individuals for the redemption of vows to God was determined by age. Individuals between the ages of five and twenty were grouped together in valuation, giving some indication that maturity comes at the age of twenty.

The Talmud is also silent with regard to a bar mitzvah at the age of thirteen, indicating that the ceremony as we have it today was unknown in Talmudic days. The Talmud, however, does mention the term bar mitzvah twice. Both times the reference is to any Jew who observes the commandments, and not necessarily to a boy at age thirteen. When referring to a boy of thirteen the Talmud uses the term *bar onshin* ("one who is punishable"). This indicates that a child in Talmudic times became liable for any wrongdoing that he may commit at age thirteen.

The clearest and most explicit recognition of thirteen as the age when a child was considered to be a fully responsible member of the community is the Mishnaic statement (Pirke Avot 5:21) that "at age thirteen one become subject to the commandments."

There is a vast array of opinions on the reason for the choice of the thirteenth year as the age for performing *mitzvot*. Some ascribe it to foreign influences present in ancient Israel in the first century B.C.E. Others feel that it may be a throwback to puberty rites that were practiced by many groups. Almost every culture in the world today has some kind of initiation rites that herald a child's entrance into puberty.

When did the "modern" bar mitzvah ceremony begin?

One of the first known scholars to use the term *bar mitzvah* in our modern sense was Mordecai ben Hillel, a German rabbi of the thirteenth century. Most references to the *bar mitzvah* appear after this date.

It was on the Sabbath after the boy's thirteenth birthday that the bar mitzvah took place. The child was called to the Torah for the very first time, often for the *maftir aliyah* (the honor of being called to the Torah with the additional honor of chanting a portion from the Prophets, the Haf-tarah). When the boy finished his *aliyah* his father would rise and say, "Blessed be God who has freed me from the responsibility for this boy." The text of the blessing, found in a midrash on Genesis (Genesis Rabbah 63:10), symbolizes the fact that from that day on the parent is no longer responsible for the child's misdeeds and that the child must now bear the responsibility for his or her own actions. This was then followed by a *seudat mitzvah* (religious meal) at which the bar mitzvah would often deliver a Bible-related talk to show what he had learned.

When did the bat mitzvah ceremony originate?

Beginning in the second or third century C.E., Jewish girls at age twelve took on legal responsibility for the performance of *mitzvot*. As with age thirteen for boys, twelve likely corre-sponded to the age of the onset of puberty. However, girls were subject to fewer commandments than the boys. They were exempted from a whole series of time-related positive commandments, on the assumption that their domestic duties at home took precedence.

Many centuries passed before the bat mitzvah ceremony appeared on the scene. In fact, the first known bat mitzvah in North America (about seventy years ago) was that of Judith Kaplan, daughter of Rabbi Mordecai Kaplan, founder of the Reconstructionist movement. The bat mitzvah was scheduled for a Friday night and Judith recited the blessings, read a section from the Bible and its English translation, and concluded with the final blessings. As time passed Conservative congregations adopted the bat mitzvah. Today it is most likely as common as the bar mitzvah and is usually held on Saturday morning.

CELEBRATING BAR/BAT MITZVAH

When are bar and bat mitzvah ceremonies held?

In most Conservative congregations bar mitzvah ceremonies are held on days that the Torah is read. This will
include Mondays, Thursdays, Saturdays, and all Jewish holidays, including *Rosh Chodesh* (the celebration of a new Jewish
month). Most Conservative congregations now permit bat
mitzvah ceremonies on all days that the Torah is read, similar
to the bar mitzvah custom. Others celebrate the bar mitzvah
on days of Torah reading but limit the celebration of the bat
mitzvah to a Friday night service.

What do the bar and bat mitzvah do in the service?

Depending on the congregation, boys and girls may conduct all or part of the service, chant the Torah blessings
and read a section or more from the Torah, recite the
Haftarah (portion from the book of the Prophets) and its
accompanying blessings, and explain in a brief speech the
significance of the Bible reading and Haftarah.

*How far in advance should a child begin to prepare for a bar
or bat mitzvah?*

The answer to this question depends upon the particular
congregation and its requirements. Most Conservative synagogues today require five years of formal religious study
along with a minimum of one year of bar/bat mitzvah
training. It is also highly advisable that bar/bat mitzvah students attend services regularly, enabling them to completely
familiarize themselves with the prayers and the customs and
rituals of their particular synagogue.

Who participates in the religious ceremony?

In addition to the bar or bat mitzvah, it is customary to have siblings, relatives, and friends of the family participate in the ceremony. Most rabbis will hold a meeting with the bar/bat mitzvah and the family several months before the ceremony. At the ceremony the rabbi will typically discuss the meaning of *mitzvot* as it relates to becoming a bar/bat mitzvah, the importance of continuing Jewish education, the theme of the Torah and Haftarah reading, and the honors available to the family. If there are non-Jewish parents and other non-Jewish relatives, the rabbi will discuss the extent of their participation as well. Since many congregations invite the parents of a Bar/Bat Mitzvah to address their child at the service, the rabbi might also discuss with them the nature of such an address, often emphasizing some important themes (trustworthy living, acceptance of *mitzvot,* and so forth) that ought to be included in their speech.

Are bar and bat mitzvah ceremonies always celebrated in the synagogue?

Most bar and bat mitzvah ceremonies are celebrated in the synagogue with which the family is affiliated. Recently a growing numbers of families have chosen to travel to Israel to celebrate their bar and bat mitzvahs. Families that choose this option often opt for some sort of celebration in their home synagogue, thus enabling all friends and relatives to attend.

What kind of party after the ceremony is appropriate?

As in all of the festive meals following Jewish rites of passage, the meal is a *seudat mitzvah* (a religious meal) and a celebration of a *simcha.* As such it takes on a special aura of sanctity. As early as the thirteenth century, local Jewish communities were concerned with parties that were overly ostentatious and with immodest displays of wealth. Accordingly community leaders often enacted special taxes to limit the size and nature of the feasts.

When planning the menu you will surely wish to consider *kashrut* so that all of the guests, both observant and not, can enjoy the meal. It is most proper to begin the meal with *hamotzi* over the bread and conclude it with the *birkat hamazon* (Blessing after the Meal). Spirited Israeli dancing can also work to invest the party with deeper Jewish feeling. It is also a nice idea to remember the less fortunate at times of such a celebration by giving a percentage of the total cost of the party to *tzedakah.* Arranging in advance to give the left over food to the needy is a *mitzvah* and a wonderful way of honoring the *bar* or *bat mitzvah.*

What if you never had a bar or bat mitzvah?

It is never to late to celebrate a bar or bat mitzvah. Numerous Conservative congregations today sponsor adult bar and bat mitzvah classes of study with their rabbis. It has been reported that members in their eighties—and even in their nineties—have availed themselves of these classes. If you did not have a bar/bat mitzvah and are prepared to undertake the necessary study, speak to your rabbi. Becoming a bar or bat mitzvah can be one of the most rewarding Jewish experiences of your adult life!

When one reaches the age of eighty three, it is customary in some congregations to allow that person the opportunity of celebrating another bar mitzvah. This can provide a wonderful opportunity for family, relatives, and friends to celebrate an important life's milestone and ought to be encouraged. In fact, as this book was being readied for publication, Judith Kaplan Eisenstein, who, as noted above, was the first known bat mitzvah, celebrated her eighty-third birthday with her second bat mitzvah celebration—but this time on *Shabbat* afternoon!

CHECKLIST FOR A BAR/BAT MITZVAH

This list will help you to keep track of the organization for your bar/bat mitzvah.

Date of bar/bat mitzvah _____

Name(s) of Torah portion and Haftarah _____

I have sent out invitations_____

Name of person with whom twinning will take place _____

Name of florist_____

Name of photographer_____

Name of caterer _____

We have selected our participants in the service and reminded those that will chant blessings to review them. They are:

Ark Openers and Closers

(English names) _____

(Hebrew names)_____

Aliyot: 1. English and Hebrew name: _____

2. English and Hebrew name: _____

3. English and Hebrew name: _____

4. English and Hebrew name: _____

5. English and Hebrew name: _____

6. English and Hebrew name: _____

7. English and Hebrew name: _____

8. Bar/Bat Mitzvah: English and Hebrew name: ___

Lift Torah: English and Hebrew name: _____

Tie Torah: English and Hebrew name:_____

_____

Other parts in service: Name _____ Part _____

Name of Kiddush chanter _____

Name of person leading *hamotzi* _____

Name of person leading *birkat hamazon* _____

List of new mitzvot that bar/bat mitzvah will consider doing the first year:

1._____

2._____

3._____

4._____

Tzedakah organizations for contributions:_____

_____

Confirmation

"It is a Tree of Life to those who hold fast to it."

HISTORICAL BACKGROUND.

When and how did confirmation originate?

The confirmation ceremony is less than two hundred years old! It was instituted in the early nineteenth century in Germany by the Reform movement. The ceremony was held at the age of sixteen instead of the bar/bat mitzvah, since the feeling was that a thirteen year old could not really be considered an adult and fully understand the significance of the religion at such a tender age.

The confirmation ceremony soon struck roots in the general Jewish community at large and has been accepted by many Conservative synagogues.

Why is confirmation generally tied to the festival of Shavuot?

In 1831, Rabbi Samuel Egers of Brunswick, Germany held his confirmation ceremony on the festival of Shavuot, the festival of the giving of the Torah on Mount Sinai. Shavuot provides the natural connection to the idea of transmitting Torah. Today the confirmation ceremonies that do take place in Conservative synagogues are generally held on the festival of Shavuot.

What are the components of a confirmation service?

There is no uniform confirmation service, nor is there a uniform standardized curriculum of preparation. In many confirmation ceremonies today that are held on Shavuot, teenagers (often tenth graders) lead various parts of the service and often perform a cantata based on the theme of reaffirmation of faith and commitment. Students often complement the traditional service with the reading of poems and personal reflections of the meaning of the event itself. Confirmation diplomas and a gift from the school to the students are often awarded at the conclusion of services.

7

Jewish Wedding

Set me as a seal upon your heart.

—Song of Songs 8:6

HISTORICAL BACKGROUND

What does Jewish tradition have to say about marriage?

It is a Jewish belief that marriage is part of the natural way of life. The Bible says that "it is not good for man to be alone. I will make a complement for him" (Genesis 2:18). God caused Adam to fall into a deep slumber and from one of his ribs God created Eve, the first woman. This biblical account concludes with the statement that "a man shall leave his father and mother and cleave to his wife and they shall become one flesh."

The Talmud reiterates that "any man who has no wife lives without joy, blessing, and goodness" (Yevamot 62b). Marriage is considered a *mitzvah,* a divine commandment. And when a Jewish couple marries it enables them to fulfil Judaism's first biblical obligation—"be fruitful and multiply."

Interestingly there is no single precise word for marriage in Hebrew. The Bible only speaks of "taking a wife." The rabbis used the Hebrew word *kiddushin* ("sanctification") to mean marriage. This word was clearly intended to express the sanctified relationship of a husband and wife. Of all of the happy events in the Jewish life cycle, Jewish marriage and the wedding is perhaps the most joyous of them all.

Who was Judaism's first matchmaker?

A well-known rabbinic parable describes a confrontation between a Roman matron and Rabbi Yose ben Chalafta. The woman asked the rabbi, "In how many days did God create the world?"

"In six days," the rabbi answered quickly.

"What has your God been doing since then?" she asked.

The rabbi replied, "God makes marriages, assigning this man to that woman, and that woman to this man."

The story goes on to tell how the matron quickly married off all of her household slaves, two by two, saying that she certainly could perform matches as well as Rabbi Yose's God. The next day the villa was filled with cries and complaints from the newly married couples. Finally the matron summoned Rabbi Yose and admitted, "There is no God like your God when it comes to making matches." In this midrash God is portrayed as the very first matchmaker. Of course other matchmakers of sorts appear throughout biblical history. One of the earliest was Abraham's trustworthy servant Eliezer, who was dispatched by his master to find a wife for Isaac, Abraham's son. The mission was successful and Rebecca was found to be the perfect match for Isaac! This ancient practice of making matches later blossomed into the institution of the *shadchan* ("matchmaker"), which will be discussed shortly.

How important was marriage in talmudic times?

The sages during talmudic times viewed marriage and child rearing as a *mitzvah*, a divine obligation. Accordingly, many talmudic passages reflect the important emphasis that the rabbis placed on the institution of Jewish marriage:

1. When a man loves his wife as himself and honors her more than himself . . . Scripture says of him: You shall know that You dwell in peace. (Yevamot 62b)
2. No man without a woman, no woman without a man, and neither without God. (Midrash Bereshit Rabbah 22:4)
3. If a husband and a wife are worthy, the Divine Presence abides with them. (Sotah 17a)

What are some guidelines for selecting a mate?

The rabbis of the Talmud encouraged people to marry and always cautioned couples to exercise the greatest of care when selecting their partners. Some of these guidelines include:

1. Hasten to buy land, but be deliberate in selecting a mate. (Yevamot 63a)
2. An old man should not marry a young woman. (Sanhedrin 76a)
3. He who weds for money shall have unworthy children. (Kiddushin 70a)
4. Do not marry a woman that you have not seen. (Kiddushin 41a)
5. Do not marry a woman for her money. (Kiddushin 70a)

Were the ancient Israelites always monogamous?

Examples of polygamy are found throughout the Bible. Our patriarch Abraham had three wives, Sarah, Hagar, and Keturah. Jacob had Leah and Rachel for his wives. King Solomon had seven hundred wives and three hundred concubines!

Most of the biblical prophets discouraged polygamy, pointing to the symbolic "marriage" of God and Israel as the ideal monogamous model. In the year 1040 C.E. Rabbenu Gershom put a stop to the possibility of polygamy among Ashkenazic Jews with his important edict. Among Sephardic and Oriental Jews the practice of polygamy has continued until recent times. In certain countries today, including Yemen in southwestern Saudia Arabia, Jews are legally permitted to have more than one wife.

What kinds of marriages are forbidden ?

In biblical times there were a number of close relatives that one was prohibited from marrying. For the most part these forbidden relationships were incestuous. A man could not marry his mother, stepmother, mother-in-law, father's or mother's sister, paternal uncle's wife, half sister, stepsister, sister-in-law, wife's sister (as long as his wife is living), daughter-in-law, stepdaughter or granddaughter (Leviticus 18:6–18). Most states in the United States today also have laws (quite similar to those set down in the Bible) that prohibit close relatives from marrying. Marriage to cousins, even first cousins, was permissible and fairly frequent. For instance, Jacob and his wives, Leah and Rachel, were cousins.

Biblical law also forbade marriage of Israelites to Canaanites. Aside from the Canaanites, the ancient Hebrews were permitted to marry outside of their people if their mate embraced Judaism. For example Boaz chose Ruth, a Moabite woman who adopted Judaism as her own.

In addition to the prohibitions mentioned in the Bible, the Talmud also placed certain restrictions on marriage partners. It forbade marriages between:

1. A man and his former wife (if she had been married to another man in the interim)
2. A Jew and a *mamzer* (child of a forbidden marriage)
3. A Jew and a *shetuki* (person of unknown parentage)
4. A woman and the only witness to her husband's death

Special restrictions regarding marriage were placed on the *Kohanim,* the ancient Priests. According to Leviticus (21:7), a *Kohen* could not marry a harlot or a divorcee. The high priest could not marry a widow. The Law Committee of the Rabbinical Assembly (the professional organization for Conservative Rabbis) ruled to allow marriages between *Kohanim* and divorcees or proselytes, with the provision that these marriages be unostentatious and that the *Kohen* would forgo his priestly privileges. The decision was based on the fact that the priestly status of most *Kohanim* is doubtful.

The Talmud also forbade Jewish weddings involving certain individuals, including:

1. Minors (boys under thirteen years and girls under the age of twelve).
2. Eunuchs, since they could not fulfil the *mitzvah* of having children.
3. Deaf and dumb men and women unless they could use sign language.
4. Incompetent persons, since they could not be assumed to fully comprehend the legal obligations of marriage.

Special restrictions were placed on second or third marriages. A widower had to observe a thirty-day mourning period before marrying again. A widow or divorcee had to wait ninety days after being divorced or widowed so that the paternity of the child could be determined.

There may well be other special situations related to forbidden relations that are not described here. For more authoritative guidance on aspects related to this subject, seek the advice of your own rabbi who will help you in this area.

What has been the status of a wife in Jewish law?

The Hebrew word for husband is *ba'al,* while the word for wife is *be'ulah.* Technically these words mean "master" and "owned one." Although technically the wife was considered "owned property," her status was one that clearly carried with it legal rights and much respect. Judaism was considered ahead of other cultures in terms of its attitude toward the treatment of women. The Bible (Exodus 21:10) specifies that a husband cannot deny his wife food, clothing, or her conjugal rights. The Talmud also specified the aforementioned support, but added other provisions, including a specified sum of money as is stipulated in the marriage contract, a provision for proper medical care, ransom money in the event of a kidnap, and a suitable burial place. Many of these obligations are taken for granted today, but Jews were among the first to provide for their women.

The biblical institution of levirate marriage also served to protect a childless widow. In the event that a man died and left no heirs, that man's brother was legally obligated to marry the widow and care for her and, it was hoped, bear children who would perpetuate the family name. Should there be no brother, the responsibility of marrying the widow lay with the closest relative. Any man who refused to perform this legal obligation was subjected to public humiliation in a ceremony known as *chalitzah* ("release") which is graphically described in Deuteronomy 25:5–10.

By the end of the biblical period, the Jewish marriage was regulated by a modicum of law and began to take on the shape of a religious and sanctified legal act.

What were the ceremonies connected with the wedding in bygone days?

Until late in the Middle Ages, there were three ceremonies connected with the Jewish wedding:

1. *Tenaim:* As soon as the matchmaker made the match, the parents of the bride and groom negotiated the terms of the marriage, including the price of the dowry. All of this was set forth in a contract called *tenaim,* which literally means "stipulations." If either party wished to break the match, a fine was imposed. The contract was sealed with the breaking of a plate. This has come to symbolize the fact that happiness in a marital relationship can be shattered as easily as the breaking of the dinner plate.

2. *Erusin:* This ceremony was the formal engagement of the
   couple. At this ceremony the *ketubah* (marriage contract)
   was written and the groom consecrated his bride by
   presenting her with a gold coin. The date for the *nisuin*
   (the actual marriage ceremony) was then set, usually to
   take place within a year of the *erusin* ceremony.
3. *Nisuin:* This was the formal marriage ceremony. From this
   time forth the couple lived together as husband and wife.
   Today the *erusin* and *nisuin* ceremonies are combined
   into one marriage service.

THE MODERN JEWISH WEDDING; PREPARATION

When may a Jewish wedding take place?

Choosing a date for a Jewish wedding can be an interesting
challenge. Jewish tradition has always placed limitations on
the choice of a wedding date. There are certain times of
the year when marriage ceremonies are forbidden. These
include the following:

1. The Sabbath and Jewish festivals, because they involve acts
   (e.g., signing the wedding *ketubah*) that are in violation
   of the Sabbath and Festival laws.
2. During the intermediate days of Passover and Sukkot,
   because of the principle that one ought not to mingle
   one joyous occasion with another.
3. During periods of national mourning, such as the days of
   the counting of the *Omer* between Passover and Shavuot,
   the "three weeks" between the seventeenth of Tammuz
   and the ninth of Av (*Tisha B'Av*).

There are many differences in practice regarding the
seven weeks of the counting of the *Omer* and the period

of the "three weeks." Because of the many variations the Committee on Jewish Law and Standards of the Rabbinical Assembly has followed the Gaonic tradition and adopted the following policy:

1. Marriages are prohibited only from the second day of Passover until Lag B'Omer. During this period marriages not accompanied by dancing, singing, and music may be performed.
2. On days during the thirty-three day period of the counting of the *Omer* when *Tachanun* (prayers of supplication) is not recited in the synagogue, as well as on Israel Independence Day (fifth of Iyyar), marriages of a public and festive nature may take place.
3. During the period of the so called "three weeks" which mark the period from the breaching of the Jerusalem walls to the destruction of the Temple, the following policy is in effect:

- Marriages are prohibited on the seventeenth of Tammuz and the ninth of Av.
- Marriages are permitted from the eighteenth of Tammuz until the last day of Tammuz.
- Small weddings (i.e., those conducted in the rabbi's study) are permitted from the first through the eighth of Av.

For many generations the selection of an auspicious wedding date was very important. The zodiac was often consulted in the hope of invoking the good spirits. It was considered good luck to marry on the new moon or as the moon was waxing in the sky—a symbol of fertility. Tuesday was a favorite day of the week on which to get married because twice on that day in the story of creation God "saw that it was good" (Genesis 1:31).

In addition to remembering when Jewish weddings cannot take place, it is also important when scheduling a wedding to take into account the schedules of the rabbi and cantor and the availability of close family and friends. Climate, the weather, and the season of the year are other variables that ought to be taken into consideration.

What are the possible choices for a Jewish wedding location?

There are no laws regarding where a wedding ceremony must take place. There are different customs and some guidelines which are worth considering. Ashkenazic and Sephardic Jews differed regarding the sites that they favored for weddings. Ashkenazim typically favored outdoor weddings, reminding them of the descendants of Abraham who were to be as numerous as the stars of the heaven (Genesis 22:17). Modern Israeli weddings also tend to be outdoors. The Sephardim, on the other hand, usually held their weddings indoors, in the synagogue.

A synagogue wedding, because of the sanctity of the sanctuary itself, can certainly add an aura of spirituality to the occasion. It becomes a place of warmth when one is a member of that particular synagogue and has likely celebrated other Jewish milestones there. The synagogue social hall, because of its convenience to all guests, is an attractive choice for the reception. Certainly, hotels and Jewish catering halls are suitable alternatives.

In cases of a smaller wedding, the home of either the bride or groom may be a fine choice. Homes are informal and can add an atmosphere of warmth and intimacy.

Who officiates at a Jewish wedding?

In Conservative Judaism now it is typically the rabbi and possibly the cantor too who act as the officiants. Of course one's own rabbi or cantor is the best choice, since they are likely to know either the bride or groom which will undoubtedly add many personal touches to the ceremony itself. It is not unusual to have both the bride and the groom represented by each family's rabbi and/or cantor. The host rabbi generally will contact the visiting clergy prior to the wedding to plan for the ceremony.

Most rabbis and cantors will typically meet with the engaged couple several months prior to the wedding to discuss the format of the ceremony and the inclusion of personal elements such as original poems, the format of the cermony, how much Hebrew in the service, where to apply for the civil license, and vows and other readings. A recommendation to be tested for Tay-Sachs disease and other genetic disorders to which some Jewish populations seem statistically susceptible may also be a part of this meeting's agenda.

The meeting itself is an excellent opportunity for the rabbi and/or cantor to become better acquainted with the couple. The couple ought to come prepared with their Hebrew names which will be needed to complete the Jewish marriage contract (*ketubah*).

What sort of clothing should the bride and groom have to purchase for their ceremony?

Jewish law does not delineate what a bride or groom must wear on their wedding day. There are, however, some interesting customs which have developed over the centuries.

The Talmud on many occasions has compared a bride and a groom to a queen and king. In talmudic times, it was not unusual to see a bride and groom seated on a thronelike chair wearing crowns as part of their costumes.

Jews in every country have developed their own customary wedding garb. In ancient Greece, both bride and groom wore white garments with garlands. Iraqi Jewish brides typically wore silver bells and golden nose rings.

North American Jewry today most commonly follows the practice that a bride wears a white gown as a sign of purity, and, often, a veil as a sign of humility and modesty. For grooms, the traditional custom was to wear a *kittel* (white robe) over his wedding suit as a symbol of purity and joy. In Conservative wedding ceremonies some grooms wear *kittels,* although it is more likely that a groom would wear a typical wedding suit. There are grooms that will also follow the custom of wearing a *tallit* at the ceremony, usually a gift from the family of the bride.

Since there are no hard-and-fast rules related to wedding dress, the most important guiding principle to keep in mind is that Judaism lauds modesty and simplicity as important principles. Wedding dresses and suits need not be extravagant to keep with our tradition!

What are the rules related to the wedding ring?

According to Jewish law, the groom must give his bride an object that has value. Many years ago the preferred object of exchange was coins. (To this day Sephardic and Oriental Jews use coins) Today in North America it is almost universally the custom to give a ring as the object of exchange. Both ancient and modern commentators have tried to explain the choice of rings. Some say that the wedding ring is a link to the past and a commitment to the future. Others say that just as a ring is circular and has no beginning and no end, so too the love of a husband and wife for each other ought to be complete and neverending.

Jewish law clearly states that every ring meet the following standards:

1. It must belong to the groom.

2. It must be of solid metal (usually gold), without precious stones. The reasoning here is that if gems were involved, there could be a substantial variation in the value among rings, and this might cause the bride to have reservations.

One ring, given by the groom to his bride, is required by Jewish law. A relatively recent custom is the double-ring ceremony, in which both bride and groom exchange rings. Some traditional authorities object to this practice since it is a deviation from tradition, especially if the statement used by the bride in the ring during the ring exchange is the same as that of the groom. The late Rabbi Isaac Klein, author of the Conservative Movement's *A Guide to Jewish Religious Practice,* has written that there can be no legal objection to double ring ceremonies. Once the traditional formula has been recited the marriage is completely binding!

It is a good idea for any engaged couple to consult with a rabbi before purchasing the ring(s).

What is the ketubah and where did it originate?

The Hebrew word *ketubah* literally means "written." It refers to the Jewish marriage contract that is signed and read at some Reform and Reconstructionist weddings and all Conservative and Orthodox ones. Historically, the *ketubah* text as we know it today came into use almost two thousand years ago. The earliest formulation was written by Shimon ben Shetach, president of the ancient rabbinic court. The important innovation of the *ketubah* is that it recognized that not only love, but legal commitment is necessary to consummate a Jewish marriage. The *ketubah* specified the husband's primary obligations to his wife. These included honoring his wife and providing her with food, clothing, and conjugal rights. The *ketubah* also specified a husband's financial obligations in the event of a divorce.

Originally all *ketubot* were written on parchment (animal skin) and often artistically illuminated in bright colors. Over the centuries each country in which Jews lived included its own cultural symbols as part of the *ketubah's* artistic design. One can arrange for a visit at the graphics department at the Library of the Jewish Theological Seminary in New York to see many examples of *ketubot* from countries the world over. In Persia, for example, the *ketubah* frequently included the lion of Judah. Many Italian *ketubot* portrayed *cherubim*. The officiating clergyperson will always provide a *ketubah* for the engaged couple. However, there is a growing trend today among couples to have a handmade *ketubah* especially designed for them by a trained calligrapher or scribe. It is important to remember that such commissions require advanced notice in order that the *ketubah* be ready on time for the wedding day.

When is the ketubah signed and by whom?

In ancient times, as today, the *ketubah* was signed just prior to the ceremony. Two witnesses are required for the signing. Jewish law requires that they be adult, religiously observant, and not related by blood or marriage to either the bride or the groom. The officiating clergy are permitted to serve as witnesses provided that they are not related to either bride or groom. Orthodox rabbis will allow only male witnesses to serve as witnesses. Reform, and some Conservative rabbis will permit women to participate. The *ketubah* is signed with complete Hebrew names, so the witnesses ought to be reminded to prepare for this requirement in advance. In addition, there are some *ketubot* that have a place for both bride and groom to sign as well. Part or all of the *ketubah* will generally be read by the officiant during the wedding ceremony itself.

What is the Lieberman ketubah formula and why is it special?

In the Conservative movement, the *ketubah* has been given a new function by the addition of a new paragraph to the additional text that was created by the late Professor Saul Lieberman, Talmudist par excellence of the Jewish Theological Seminary. In 1955 the following clause by Lieberman was added to the *ketubah*:

> And in solemn assent to their mutual responsibilities of love, the bridegroom and bride have declared: As evidence of our desire to enable each other to live in accordance with the Jewish Law of Marriage throughout our lifetime, we, the bride and bridegroom, attach our signature to this *ketubah* and hereby agree to recognize the *Bet Din* of the Rabbinical Assembly of America or its duly appointed representatives, as having authority to counsel us in the light of Jewish tradition which requires husband and wife to give each other complete love and devotion and to summon either party at the request of the other, in order to enable the party so requesting to live in accordance with the standards of the Jewish Law of Marriage throughout his or her lifetime. We authorize the *Bet Din* to impose such terms of compensation as it may see fit for failure to respond to its summons or to carry out its decisions.

This new clause represented a private agreement between the bride and groom entered upon prior to their marriage. It was intended to open up the possibility of bringing a civil action against a recalcitrant husband who refused to comply with the terms of his wife's *ketubah*. It is still uncertain whether the courts will in fact enforce the agreement, since civil courts tend to shun cases involving religious obligations.

What is a chuppah and what does it symbolize?

The *chuppah* is the wedding canopy under which the bride

and groom stand during the ceremony. It is a symbolic marriage chamber, indicative of the bride leaving her father's house and entering her husband's domain as a married woman.

In biblical times the meaning of the word *chuppah* was "room" or "covering." The Book of Joel (2:16) states: "Let the bridegroom go forth from his chamber and the bride out of her pavilion (*chuppah*)."

In Israel there was a custom to plant a cedar tree on the occasion of a child's birth. When the child married, the branches and leaves from the tree were used for the poles and decorative materials for the *chuppah.*

Today the *chuppah* is usually a canopy supported by four staves which can be held by friends or relatives of the bride and groom during the ceremony itself. It can be a decorated cloth or even a *tallit* (prayer shawl). In Sephardic ceremonies the *tallit* itself is actually draped over the head of both bride and groom before the wedding ceremony begins.

Most Conservative synagogues and catering halls have their own *chuppah,* which is often decorated by a florist. Some even have several *chuppah* styles to choose from. It is sensible for any engaged couple to check on the details of their *chuppah* in advance so that it will properly meet with their approval and allow for any adjustments to be made.

What kind of music is suitable for the wedding procession?

Music has always been a part of Jewish tradition. In biblical times marriage processions were often accompanied by musicians, and in talmudic times there were even rabbis who would lead the wedding guests in responsive singing!

Since there are only guidelines concerning the choice of music for a wedding procession, the couple has much flexibility in choosing what is appropriate for them. Most rabbis will provide a couple at their "getting-to-know you" meeting with some appropriate possibilities. Cantors, too, will surely be able to serve as advisors. Their choices will usually include Jewish folk, liturgical, and modern melodies which can transform the ceremonial processional into a beautiful sanctified experience. Many rabbis and cantors will also express to the couple those musical choices which they feel ought to be avoided. "Here Comes the Bride," for example, is usually on the not-to-be used list, having been composed by Richard Wagner, a known anti-Semite.

There is also a range of possibilities for the music at the wedding reception. Rabbis and cantors will usually suggest the inclusion of Israeli and traditional Jewish wedding dances. They tend to be very participatory and engaging to almost everyone present at the reception. In recent years there has also been a resurgence of interest in klezmer bands which play Eastern European music. This type of instrumental music can also add a traditional Jewish flavor to any wedding celebration.

What are tenaim?

The *tenaim* (literally "conditions") date to the third century C.E. In talmudic times, as soon as a marital match was arranged, the parents of the bride and groom negotiated a number of things. Among the items discussed were the size of the dowry (the money and other possessions that the bride would bring to the marriage), the *mohar* or "bride price" (the value in money or services that the groom would pay to the bride's father for the privilege of marrying his daughter), and the penalty in fines that would be paid if either party failed to fulfil its promises. When all of the conditions were agreed upon, a document known as the *tenaim* was drawn up. A china dish was broken to seal the agreement.

Although some couples today in Conservative settings still

practice the custom of writing a *tenaim* document, it is no longer very popular. The engagement ring and engagement party has become a sort of modern-day substitute for the *tenaim* ritual. Some couples have reinterpreted the custom of *tenaim* by writing a prenuptial agreement, which might typically include the desired number of children, financial matters, and so forth.

What is an aufruf?

Aufruf is a German word meaning "calling up." It refers to a synagogue celebration usually held on the Sabbath preceding the wedding. The custom is ascribed to the Bible. King Solomon had his attendants perform deeds of kindness for a groom on the Sabbath preceding his wedding day. Today an *aufruf* gives communal recognition to a forthcoming marriage.

The *aufruf* is usually scheduled on the Sabbath immediately prior to the wedding. If that particular Sabbath is inconvenient for the family of the bride and groom, an earlier one can be chosen. If a bride and groom's family is not affiliated with a synagogue, a suitable arrangement can usually be made by calling the local congregation.

At the *aufruf* it is customary for the groom to be called to the Torah for an *aliyah*. In many Conservative synagogues, both bride and groom share the *aliyah*. It may also be customary to offer Torah honors to honor family members, including parents or grandparents, aunts and uncles. When the groom (and bride) are called up to the Torah, the following is recited.

בָּרְכוּ אֶת יְיָ הַמְבֹרָךְ.

Barechu et Adonai ham'vorach.

בָּרוּךְ יְיָ הַמְבֹרָךְ לְעוֹלָם וָעֶד.

Baruch Adonai ham'vorach l'olam va- ed.

The person repeats the response and continues:

בָּרוּךְ אַתָּה, יְיָ אֱלֹהֵינוּ, מֶלֶךְ הָעוֹלָם, אֲשֶׁר בָּחַר בָּנוּ מִכָּל הָעַמִּים, וְנָתַן לָנוּ אֶת תּוֹרָתוֹ. בָּרוּךְ אַתָּה יְיָ, נוֹתֵן הַתּוֹרָה.

Baruch ata Adonai elohenu melech ha-olam asher bachar banu mikol ha-amim, v'natan lahnu et torato. Baruch ata Adonai, notayn ha-torah.

When Torah portion is completed:

בָּרוּךְ אַתָּה, יְיָ אֱלֹהֵינוּ, מֶלֶךְ הָעוֹלָם, אֲשֶׁר נָתַן לָנוּ תּוֹרַת אֱמֶת, וְחַיֵּי עוֹלָם נָטַע בְּתוֹכֵנוּ. בָּרוּךְ אַתָּה יְיָ, נוֹתֵן הַתּוֹרָה.

Baruch ata adonai elohenu melech ha-olam asher natan lanu torat emet v'chayeh olam natah b'tochaynu. Baruch ata adonai, notayn ha-torah.

After the aliyah has been completed the rabbi often recites a prayer on behalf of the couple:

> May God who blessed our ancestors, Abraham, Isaac, Jacob, Sarah, Rebecca, Rachel, and Leah, bless _____ and his bride _____ who are soon to be married. May they together build a Jewish home harboring love and harmony, peace and friendship. May they be blessed with children reared in good health and well-being, devoted to Torah and to good deeds.

Some congregations follow the old custom of throwing candy and nuts after the *aliyah* or after the rabbi blesses the couple. These foods symbolize the community's good wishes to the couple for a sweet and prosperous life. This may be followed by the spirited singing of *Siman tov u'mazal tov*, again wishing the couple good fortune.

At the conclusion of services, it is customary for the family of the bride and groom to invite the entire congregation to a *kiddush* (refreshments). In this way everyone can happily share in the celebration while at the same time fulfilling the important Jewish *mitzvah* of hospitality.

What is a mikvah?

It has been customary for the bride, prior to her wedding, to immerse in the *mikvah* (ritual bath). This immersion was intended to prepare her to enter marriage in a state of physical and mental purity. Some grooms would also visit the *mikvah* in the morning of the wedding or the Friday afternoon preceding it. With all of the many demands made upon a prospective bride and groom prior to their wedding day, it is very easy to forget the important spiritual act of immersion. The rabbi is a good person to speak to regarding the *mikvah* experience and procedure.

What are some other spiritual preparations for a bride and groom to consider?

A recent custom is the separation of the bride and groom during the week before the wedding. The intent of this custom was most likely to heighten the anticipation of seeing each other on their wedding day and to provide an opportunity to reflect about the major step they were about to take. In addition, it would allow both bride and groom to spend some additional private time with their respective families.

Giving *tzedakah* (charity) as a thanksgiving offering is often associated with weddings. More and more often, brides and grooms are arranging in advance to donate flowers and left-over food from their reception to the needy and the sick. Another beautiful custom is the donation of the bridal gown for use by brides who may not be able to afford their own.

THE WEDDING DAY

We now have come to the actual wedding day itself. Many of the customs and rituals for this special day have emerged over the many centuries.

What is the custom of fasting on the wedding day?

It has long been customary for both the bride and the groom to fast on their wedding day until the marriage ceremony. The custom originated in medieval Germany, and many reasons for it have been advanced. Some say that fasting gives the wedding day a solemnity that prevents cheap merrymaking from taking place. Others connect the custom to the celebration of Yom Kippur, where fasting is designed to cleanse one's soul. So too, abstaining from food on one's wedding day symbolizes a new beginning and the cleansing of all of one's past transgressions. The fast of the bride and groom will officially end when the couple share their first cup of wine under the *chuppah* during the actual ceremony.

What are some customs before the ceremony begins?

Many Conservative rabbis will ask that the bride and groom be in separate quarters before the ceremony itself begins. This tends to heighten the anticipation of seeing each other. Each stays with his or her own entourage of special friends whose task it is to make the bride and groom "comfortable" and keep them relaxed.

First, the *ketubah* will be signed. The rabbi will enter the room where the groom is situated with the two witnesses. The rabbi will then ask the groom to take hold of a kerchief extended to him and explain that by doing so he agrees to be bound by the conditions specified in the *ketubah*. (This brief ceremony is called *kabalat kinyan*) The two witnesses then will sign their names to the *ketubah*.

There are variations among Conservative rabbis related to the signing of the *ketubah*. Some will have both bride and groom sign, each in separate rooms and each in the presence of the same two witnesses. Some will perform the above with both bride and groom in the same room. The civil marriage license will also be signed at this time. (Note: This license can be signed by any adult, male or female, of the bride or groom's choosing.) Of course the same two witnesses that signed the *ketubah* could also be used for the civil document as well. The customs related to the signing of the *ketubah* will usually be discussed with the couple in advance by the officiant at the ceremony.

What is the badeken ceremony?

Badeken is the veiling ceremony. The custom of a bride wearing a veil is often ascribed to the biblical story about Rebecca. When she saw Isaac for the first time, "she took the veil and covered herself" (Genesis 24:65). Thus the veil has become a sign of modesty and humility. According to still another interpretation, the veiling ceremony developed to prevent a recurrence of what happened to Jacob in biblical times. Laban, Rachel's father, tricked the groom Jacob by substituting his older daughter Leah, who wore a veil. In order to avoid future dilemmas such as this, it has become customary for the groom to personally lower the veil over his bride's face.

The veiling ceremony takes place just before the wedding

ceremony is to commence. It often will take place in an area where all of the guests are able to see the ceremony. The groom is instructed to place the veil over his bride's face. This is followed by the groom, or the bride's father, or sometimes even the officiant, pronouncing the blessings bestowed upon Rebecca before she left home (Genesis 24:6):

אֲחֹתֵנוּ אַתְּ הֲיִי לְאַלְפֵי רְבָבָה.

O sister! May you grow into thousands of myriads.

This blessing is often followed by the priestly blessing.

יְשִׂימֵךְ אֱלֹהִים כְּשָׂרָה רִבְקָה רָחֵל וְלֵאָה.

Yiseemech eloheem k'Sarah Rivka Rachel v'Leah

May God make you as Sarah, Rebekah, Rachel and Leah.

יְבָרֶכְךָ יְיָ וְיִשְׁמְרֶךָ,
יָאֵר יְיָ פָּנָיו אֵלֶיךָ וִיחֻנֶּךָּ.
יִשָּׂא יְיָ פָּנָיו אֵלֶיךָ וְיָשֵׂם לְךָ שָׁלוֹם.

Yevarechecha Adonai v'yishmerecha
Ya'er Adonai Panav Eylecha Veechuneka,
Yisa Adonai Panav Eylecha Veyasem Lecha Shalom.

May God bless you and keep you
May God's Presence shine and be good to you.
May God's face turn toward you and give you peace.

The wedding ceremony is now ready to begin.

Who are the members of the wedding processional?

It is an ancient custom to escort the bride and groom to the *chuppah*. An early midrash describes God as having personally escorted Eve to Adam. Usually it is customary for parents, grandparents, sisters, brothers, and close friends to be a part of those who march down the aisle.

The actual order of the procession and the number of participants is not fixed by Jewish law. A number of customs, though, have emerged which may serve as useful guides. It is most usual for both the bride and groom to be escorted by their parents. The role of best man and maid or matron of honor also has an early precedent. The midrash reports that Michael and Gabriel, two ministering angels, attended the wedding of Adam and Eve. The bride and groom's friends or siblings would make suitable honorees for best man, maid of honor, or ring bearer. Grandparents may also join in the processional. In some processionals, the participants hold candles. It has been said that the candles are reminders of the lightning that was experienced on the day that the Torah was given to the Jewish people and God bonded himself to the people of Israel.

At the conclusion of the ceremony the bride and groom usually leave first, followed in reverse order by all of those who participated in the wedding processional.

Some couples may hold a rehearsal a few days before the wedding. Most rabbis today will suggest that a lengthy rehearsal prior to the wedding day is not necessary. A brief rehearsal on the day of the wedding ceremony will more than suffice.

What are the parts of the wedding ceremony and what do they mean?

1. Circling the Groom: There is a custom for the bride to circle the groom seven times (an alternative custom is three times). The bride then stands under the *chuppah* on the right of the groom. The origin of this custom is unclear. Some believe that its purpose was to ward off

evil spirits. Others saw the number seven as symbolizing perfection, since the world was created in seven days. The preference of three circles is based on the following biblical verses "And I will betroth you to me forever. I will betroth you to me in righteousness, and in justice, and in lovingkindness, and in compassion, and I will betroth you to me in faithfulness" (Hosea 2:21–22).

Although there are still brides in Conservative Judaism that perform the circling custom, many others choose not to follow the custom because of its magical connotations.

2. Many rabbis begin the formal wedding ceremony by welcoming the bride and groom and all of the guests:

בָּרוּךְ הַבָּא בְּשֵׁם יְיָ.

Baruch haba beshem Adonai

May you who are here be blessed in the name of God.

3. *Erusin* (Betrothal blessings) Wine has always been associated with Jewish celebrations. It is Judaism's most festive beverage. In this part of the ceremony, called *erusin,* two blessings are chanted over a first cup of wine. (A second cup will be used shortly for the *sheva berachot.*) The *erusin* blessings are:

בָּרוּךְ אַתָּה יְיָ אֱלֹהֵינוּ מֶלֶךְ הָעוֹלָם, בּוֹרֵא פְּרִי הַגָּפֶן.
בָּרוּךְ אַתָּה יְיָ אֱלֹהֵינוּ מֶלֶךְ הָעוֹלָם, אֲשֶׁר קִדְּשָׁנוּ בְּמִצְוֹתָיו
וְצִוָּנוּ עַל הָעֲרָיוֹת, וְאָסַר לָנוּ אֶת־הָאֲרוּסוֹת, וְהִתִּיר לָנוּ אֶת־
הַנְּשׂוּאוֹת לָנוּ עַל יְדֵי חֻפָּה וְקִדּוּשִׁין. בָּרוּךְ אַתָּה יְיָ, מְקַדֵּשׁ
עַמּוֹ יִשְׂרָאֵל עַל יְדֵי חֻפָּה וְקִדּוּשִׁין.

Blessed be You, Adonai our God, Ruler of the universe, who createst the fruit of the vine.

Praised be You, Adonai, who hallows Your people Israel with the *chuppah* and the rites of matrimony.

The bride and groom are now asked to share in drinking from the first cup of wine, symbolically affirming that throughout their life they will experience sweetness together.

Next, the groom places the ring on his bride's right index finger. This finger has been traditionally chosen because it is the most prominent and can be easily seen by the two witnesses. Following the ceremony the ring may be moved to the more usual ring finger.

As the groom places the ring on his bride's finger, he recites these traditional words of consecration:

הֲרֵי אַתְּ מְקֻדֶּשֶׁת לִי בְּטַבַּעַת זוֹ כְּדַת מֹשֶׁה וְיִשְׂרָאֵל.

Haray at m'kudeshet li b'taba'at zoh k'dat moshe v'yisrael.

By this ring you are consecrated to me as my wife in accordance with the Law of Moses and the people of Israel.

In a double-ring ceremony, the bride then gives her groom a ring and might recite:

הֲרֵי אַתָּה מְקֻדָּשׁ לִי בְּטַבַּעַת זוֹ כְּדַת מֹשֶׁה וְיִשְׂרָאֵל.

Haray atah m'kudash li b'taba'at zoh k'dat moshe v'yisrael.

By this ring you are consecrated to me as my husband in accordance with the Law of Moses and the people of Israel.
or (Song of Songs 6:3)

אֲנִי לְדוֹדִי וְדוֹדִי לִי

Ani ledodi vedodi li

I am my beloved's and my beloved is mine.

Some couples will choose to add a poem or a personal statement during the exchange of rings. This possibility will often be discussed in advance with the rabbi.

The ring ceremony completes the first part of the wedding ceremony. Although there are no formal vows in the Jewish wedding liturgy, some rabbis do choose to include them immediately following the ceremony of the ring(s):

> Do you, _____, take _____. to be your husband/bride, promising to protect and cherish him/her, whether in good fortune or in adversity, and to seek together a life hallowed by the faith of Israel?

Some Conservative rabbis will often permit the recitation of original vows of bride and groom, if they so desire.

Next, the rabbi will generally read a portion or all of the *ketubah*. It is then given to the groom, who gives it to the bride. The bride may then choose to give it to her parents or maid of honor for safekeeping until the ceremony is completed.

After the reading of the *ketubah,* some rabbis choose to speak to both bride and groom. The talk may be a message about Jewish marriage in general, although it will tend to become more anecdotal and personal when the rabbi is well acquainted with the couple.

4. *Kiddushin* (Sanctification): The recitation of the *sheva berachot* ("seven blessings") is at the heart of this part of the Jewish wedding ceremony called *kiddushin.* These blessings may be recited by the rabbi or cantor. Sometimes close friends or relatives of the bride or groom are invited to recite the blessings, providing a nice personal touch! Among the themes of the *sheva berachot* are

gratitude to God for making man in God's image, and a request of God to grant the same joy to bride and groom as was given to Adam and Eve in the Garden of Eden.

בָּרוּךְ אַתָּה יְיָ אֱלֹהֵינוּ מֶלֶךְ הָעוֹלָם, בּוֹרֵא פְּרִי הַגָּפֶן.

בָּרוּךְ אַתָּה יְיָ אֱלֹהֵינוּ מֶלֶךְ הָעוֹלָם, שֶׁהַכֹּל בָּרָא לִכְבוֹדוֹ.

בָּרוּךְ אַתָּה יְיָ אֱלֹהֵינוּ מֶלֶךְ הָעוֹלָם, יוֹצֵר הָאָדָם.

בָּרוּךְ אַתָּה יְיָ אֱלֹהֵינוּ מֶלֶךְ הָעוֹלָם, אֲשֶׁר יָצַר אֶת־הָאָדָם בְּצַלְמוֹ, בְּצֶלֶם דְּמוּת תַּבְנִיתוֹ, וְהִתְקִין לוֹ מִמֶּנּוּ בִּנְיַן עֲדֵי עַד. בָּרוּךְ אַתָּה יְיָ, יוֹצֵר הָאָדָם.

שׂוֹשׂ תָּשִׂישׂ וְתָגֵל הָעֲקָרָה בְּקִבּוּץ בָּנֶיהָ לְתוֹכָהּ בְּשִׂמְחָה. בָּרוּךְ אַתָּה יְיָ, מְשַׂמֵּחַ צִיּוֹן בְּבָנֶיהָ.

שַׂמֵּחַ תְּשַׂמַּח רֵעִים הָאֲהוּבִים. כְּשַׂמֵּחֲךָ יְצִירְךָ בְּגַן עֵדֶן מִקֶּדֶם. בָּרוּךְ אַתָּה יְיָ, מְשַׂמֵּחַ חָתָן וְכַלָּה.

בָּרוּךְ אַתָּה יְיָ אֱלֹהֵינוּ מֶלֶךְ הָעוֹלָם, אֲשֶׁר בָּרָא שָׂשׂוֹן וְשִׂמְחָה, חָתָן וְכַלָּה, גִּילָה רִנָּה דִּיצָה וְחֶדְוָה, אַהֲבָה וְאַחֲוָה וְשָׁלוֹם וְרֵעוּת. מְהֵרָה יְיָ אֱלֹהֵינוּ יִשָּׁמַע בְּעָרֵי יְהוּדָה וּבְחוּצוֹת יְרוּשָׁלַיִם קוֹל שָׂשׂוֹן וְקוֹל שִׂמְחָה, קוֹל חָתָן וְקוֹל כַּלָּה, קוֹל מִצְהֲלוֹת חֲתָנִים מֵחֻפָּתָם וּנְעָרִים מִמִּשְׁתֵּה נְגִינָתָם. בָּרוּךְ אַתָּה יְיָ, מְשַׂמֵּחַ חָתָן עִם הַכַּלָּה.

Praised are You, Adonai, our God, Guide of the universe, Creator of the fruit of the vine.

Praised are You, Adonai, our God, Guide of the universe, who created all things for Your glory.

Praised are You, Adonai, our God, Guide of the universe, Creator of human beings.

Praised are You, Adonai, our God, Guide of the universe, who creates man and woman in Your image, fashioning woman from man as his partner. Praised are You, Creator of human beings.

May Zion be happy as her children are restored to joy. Praised are You, Adonai, who causes Zion to be happy at her children's return.

Grant perfect joy to these loving companions, as You did to the first man and woman in the Garden of Eden. Praised are You, Adonai, who grants happiness to bride and groom.

Praised are You, Adonai, our God, Guide of the universe, who creates joy and gladness, bride and groom, happiness, delight, rejoicing, love and harmony, peace and friendship. May there be heard in the cities of Judah and the streets of Jerusalem voices of joy and happiness, bride and groom, the jubilant voices of those joined in marriage under the *chuppah*, the voices of young people feasting and singing. Praised are You, Adonai, who causes the groom to be happy with his bride.

The bride and groom now sip from the second cup of wine.

Some rabbis end the wedding ceremony with the official pronouncement: "By the power vested in me in the state of ___ you are now husband and wife." Others bless the bride and groom with the threefold priestly benediction:

יְבָרֶכְךָ יְיָ וְיִשְׁמְרֶךָ,
יָאֵר יְיָ פָּנָיו אֵלֶיךָ וִיחֻנֶּךָּ,
יִשָּׂא יְיָ פָּנָיו אֵלֶיךָ וְיָשֵׂם לְךָ שָׁלוֹם.

May God bless you and keep you
May God deal kindly and graciously with you.
May God bestow favor upon you and grant you peace.

5. Breaking of the Glass: The wedding ceremony ends with the customary breaking of the glass. The shattering of a glass provides a most sudden mood reversal. There are numerous explanations for this custom. Some connect it with the destruction of the Temple, reminding us that even in time of great joy we must never forget our people's suffering throughout history. Others take it as a reminder that marriage is as fragile as glass.

These sober reflections last for only an instant, for after the glass is broken by the groom, greetings of *mazal tov,* shouts of joy and jubilant music often break forth as the newly married couple leave the *chuppah.*

6. *Yichud* (Unchaperoned togetherness): Following the recessional, bride and groom will often share a few quiet moments together alone. This ceremony actually began in ancient times when the groom brought his bride to his tent to consummate the marriage. Today, couples will often share some food together, their first meal as husband and wife.

POST WEDDING CELEBRATIONS

What are the religious observances related to the wedding reception?

As previously mentioned, the Bible provides little information about wedding ceremonies—a man simply took a wife. We do know, however, that when Jacob married Leah, all the people gathered together for a nuptial feast. No other details are recorded.

The celebration after a Jewish rite of passage, particularly a wedding, is truly an occasion of great joy. The festive meal itself is called a *Seudat Mitzvah,* a religious meal celebrating the observance of a religious commandment. The Talmud tells us even the studying of Torah can be interrupted so that people can bring joy and honor to the newlyweds.

Many Jewish customs and traditions have evolved through the years that help ensure that every bride and groom would fully experience the spiritual ecstasy inherent in every Jewish wedding. At the wedding reception, singing, dancing, jesting, and merrymaking are the rule. Bride and groom are often lifted in their chairs and carried around like a queen and king on thrones. At many wedding receptions it has become customary for the family to join in a "*mitzvah* dance," while holding a handkerchief between them.

Of course the wedding reception ought to begin with the *hamotzi* prayer over the bread. Traditionally it is ended with the recitation of the Grace after Meals, the *Birkat HaMazon*. In the special Grace for weddings, the seven wedding blessings (*sheva berachot*) recited under the *chuppah* are recited once again. Friends of the bride and groom are often honored with the recitation of these blessings. Two cups of wine are then poured together into a third cup, from which the bride and groom both drink. This sharing is symbolic of the joining of their lives together and their becoming the newest Jewish family.

It is nice to remember the less fortunate at times of celebration. Many couples arrange to share their flowers with hospital patients and left-over food with food banks.

What are some other post-marriage Jewish customs?

In days gone by, brides and grooms would spend the first week of their married life surrounded by relatives and friends who fed and entertained them. This custom may have originated with the biblical seven day banquet prepared by Laban for Jacob and Leah. In modern times, it is still customary to entertain the couple nightly and to chant the seven blessings of consecration whenever the bride and groom dine.

Since biblical times, the special status of a bride and groom lasted for one entire year! The Book of Deuteronomy (24:5) specifies this: "When a man takes a wife, he shall be deferred from military duty . . . He shall be free for his house one year and shall cheer his wife whom he has taken." Since the first year of any newlywed's life presents a host of adjustments and new decisions, Judaism's advice is clearly to have them stay home and learn to build and solidify a relationship of respect, cooperation, and togetherness.

CHECKLIST FOR A JEWISH WEDDING

This list will help you to keep track of your wedding plans.

Wedding date _____

Officiants _____

Place of wedding _____

Place of reception _____

Our meeting with the rabbi/cantor will take place on ____

We have selected our wedding ring(s)

We have ordered our wedding invitations

We have chosen our wedding clothes

We have selected our *chuppah*

We have selected our *ketubah*

Our two witnesses will be_____

Our attendants will be: Best man: _____

Maid/matron of honor_____

Other attendants in our wedding procession are:_____

_____

We have chosen the musical selections _____

We have taken our blood tests and applied for the civil

license _____

We have arranged for an *aufruf*_____

We have arranged for an organization that will use food left

over from the reception _____

The organization(s) to which we will contribute *tzedakah*

include_____

8

Divorce

When a man divorces his wife, even the Altar sheds tears
—Gittin 90b

*H*ISTORICAL BACKGROUND

Judaism exalts the sanctity of marriage and family life. Marriage is seen as the ideal state in Jewish tradition, part of the natural way of life. Yet, centuries ago, our ancestors recognized the possibility that a marital relationship could fail, that two people may not be able to stay and live with each other. Accordingly, provisions were made for the possibility of divorce in biblical times. "A man takes a wife and possesses her. She fails to please him because he finds something obnoxious about her, and he writes her a bill of divorcement, hands it to her, and sends her away from his house; she leaves his household and becomes the wife of another man . . ." (Deuteronomy 24:1–2). Though no specific divorcing couple is mentioned in the Torah, it is clear that the practice existed and that the Israelites had developed a legal means of handling what was often a difficult and painful situation.

What does the Talmud have to say about divorce?

There is an entire Talmudic tractate called *"Gittin* ("Divorces") which elaborates upon the specific details related to the divorce procedure. Talmudic law required the giving of a *get* (divorce document) when any marriage between two Jews ended, whether or not a religious wedding ceremony had taken place.

Technically speaking, Jewish law provided for a divorce action inititiated by the husband, since it was always the husband who "gave" the *get.* In practice, however, the Jewish court on occasion could force a husband to give his wife a divorce under certain circumstances.

A debate between the two famous rabbinic schools of Hillel and Shammai dealt with this issue. Shammai held that adultery was the only valid reason for divorce, while Hillel said that any reason was sufficient. The law of the Talmud followed the school of Hillel, resulting in a husband being allowed to divorce his wife "at will."

There were a number of specific talmudic guidelines on grounds of divorce. For example, the law provided that a man could divorce his wife (a) if she refuses conjugal relations, (b) if she has no children after having been married ten years, (c) if she commits adultery, (d) if she is lax in religious observance.

On the other hand, the Jewish court could force a husband to give his wife a divorce (a) if he refused her conjugal relations, (b) if he was cruel to her, (c) if he converted to another faith, (d) he was lax in religious observance, or (e) if he refused her support (clothing, food, and shelter).

DIVORCE PROCEEDINGS

Who requires a get?

According to Jewish law, a *get* (bill of divorce) is required for every Jewish divorce, whether or not there was a religious wedding ceremony. The sole exception is an interfaith marriage of a Jew to a non-Jew, which is not considered valid in the view of Jewish law and therefore requires no *get*. Conservative rabbis require a *get* from a prior marriage as a precondition for officiating at a wedding.

What does a get look like?

Originally the *get* was a document of twelve lines, written in Hebrew and Aramaic in Torah script with a quill pen on parchment. Nowadays heavy white paper is often used in lieu of parchment. The twelve lines on a *get* correspond to the twelve lines of empty space separating the first four books of the Torah.

Each *get* contains the following components:

1. A statement that the husband divorces his wife without duress.
2. A statement that after the *get* the husband and wife may have no further sexual relationship.
3. The time and place of the writing of the *get*.
4. Complete Hebrew names of husband and wife, including any nicknames or added names by which they may be known.

Who writes the get?

Any Jew is legally allowed to write a *get*. Since a *get* has so many complex rules, it has become customary today to have the *get* written by a *sofer* (a qualified Jewish scribe) who has the specific expertise in this area. In recent years there has been a shortage of qualified scribes. The Jewish Theological Seminary of America has responded to this need by offering summer courses in Divorce Proceedings. The graduates of this program are authorized to write a *get* and have provided many communities with an expertise which has been desperately needed.

Who are the witnesses at a Jewish divorce proceeding?

According to Jewish law, the witnesses must not be related to the wife or the husband, to each other, or to the officiating rabbi, and they should be pious, reliable, and of good repute. This applies both to the witnesses who sign the *get* and to the witnesses who are present when it is delivered.

What is the nature of the divorce proceedings?

To a certain degree, the ritual of giving and receiving a *get* is a sort of reversal of the Jewish wedding ceremony.

The entire procedure may take from one to two hours. The majority of the time is taken up by the actual writing of the *get* by the scribe.

Both husband and wife are asked a number of routine questions to ascertain their free will and consent in the divorce action. For example, the rabbi will begin by asking the husband: "Do you, _____ [name of husband] give this *get* of your own free will without duress or compulsion." After the give and take of questions and answers, the rabbi tells the wife to remove all her jewelry from her hands, and to hold her hands together with open palms upward in a position to receive the *get*. The scribe folds the *get* and gives it to the rabbi. The rabbi gives the *get* to the husband, who, holding it in both hands, drops it into the palms of the wife and says: "This be your *get*, and with it you are divorced from me from this time forth so that you may become the wife of any man." The wife then receives the *get*, lifts up her hands, walks with the *get* a short distance and returns. She then gives the *get* to the rabbi who again reads it with the witnesses. After the proceedings are completed, a tear is made in the *get* to indicate that it has been used and cannot be used again. The document itself is retained by the *Bet Din* and kept in a permanent file. Official letters, called a release, or *petor,* in Hebrew, are given to the husband and wife to certify that their marriage was dissolved according to Jewish law.

Are there any other new ceremonies to mark the end of a Jewish marriage?

In recent months several new ceremonies (taking place following the traditional ceremony) have begun to emerge. Many have resulted from the lack of compassion and experience of loneliness that women have expressed feeling while immersed in the traditional ceremony, and their need for additional emotional support. Some women have suggested that bringing a good friend to the actual presentation of the *get* would be a great help. Some of the common elements and symbols that these new ceremonies have shared include salt water (symbolizing tears), an egg (symbolizing both sadness and regeneration), and a blessing over wine (symbolizing reaffirmation of faith). It is likely in the years to come that additional customs and rituals will continue to emerge as a support for the divorced couple.

What is the delivery of a get through an agent?

If the wife is not present when the get is written, the husband may appoint an agent (called a *shaliach*) to deliver the *get,* or, if this is not feasible, the husband may authorize this agent to appoint yet another agent to deliver the *get* to his wife. The wife may also appoint an agent to act on her behalf in receiving the *get* from her husband.

How soon after the get is given may the couple remarry?

Jewish law states that the husband may remarry at once, whereas the wife is required to wait at least ninety-two days so that the paternity of any possible pregnancy will not be in question.

9

Conversion

Dearer to God is the proselyte who has come of his own accord than all the crowds of Israelites who stood before Mount Sinai ...

—Tanchuma, ed. Buber, Lech Lecha 6 f., 32a

BACKGROUND

It is estimated that over ten thousand persons convert to Judaism in the United States each year. This number is unprecedented in modern history. Many of these conversions will occur prior to a marriage or after a marriage but prior to the birth of children. This is precipitated by a desire for family togetherness and a need to share every aspect of life with the people they love. There are also those who will choose Judaism because of the personal conviction that it provides the most meaningful way of life.

What are the biblical references to proselytes?

During the biblical period, prior to the destruction of the Temple, the concept of conversion did not really exist. When Israelite men married non-Israelite women, they expected their wives to learn to worship the God of the Israelites and to become full members of the tribes—and the wives did become members of the tribe. Similarly, when Israelite women married non-Israelite men, they joined their husband's tribe.

The Bible records many mixed marriages. David, Solomon, and Moses married non-Israelite women. Boaz married a Moabite woman named Ruth. In the biblical book carrying her name, Ruth decides that she wants to become a part of her mother-in-law Naomi's people. She says: "Entreat me not to leave you, for wherever you go, I will go, and wherever you lodge, I will lodge. Your people will be my people, and your God will be my God" (Ruth 1:16). In this powerful statement Ruth chooses to be an Israelite. Later in the book she marries an Israelite named Boaz. They have a child named Obed who will later become the father of Jesse, who is the father of King David. It is amazing that King David, then, is the great-grandson of Ruth, a convert! What's more, we are taught that the Messiah will descend from King David, and, therefore, also from a convert (Bereshit Rabbah 97).

The Hebrew word for convert is *ger,* which in biblical times meant "resident alien." A resident alien was a non-Israelite who lived in Israel and was respectful of God but had no political rights. The Bible is filled with admonitions to the Israelites to treat the *ger* well, for at one time all Israelites were *gerim* (plural of *ger*) in Egypt and we must remember our suffering there.

When did the first conversions occur?

The first conversions occurred during the Babylon Exile (6th century B.C.E.) Many people were attracted to the Jewish religion and became part of the Jewish people, even if they did not live in Israel. The prophet Isaiah referred to them as "those who joined themselves to the Lord" (Isaiah 56:3–7) and promised them that they would be a part of the historic return to Zion.

After the rebuilding of the Temple, Jews engaged in extensive proselytization. Even Roman nobility converted to Judaism. So too did Queen Helena of Adiabene and all of her royal family!

What are some talmudic attitudes toward proselytes?

The attitude of the Talmud toward conversion and proselytes is varied. In the tractate Yevamot (47b) is a statement that "proselytes are as hard for Israel as a sore." On the other hand, in another place (Gerim 4:3), we find the statement "Beloved are proselytes by God, for the Bible everywhere uses the same epithet of them as of Israel."

The reason proselytes were held in such high regard is expressed in the midrash: "The Holy One loves proselytes exceedingly. We likewise should show favor to the proselyte who left his family, his father's house, his people, and all the gentile peoples of the world, and came to us. He therefore deserves special protection" (Bamidbar Rabbah 8:2).

The following midrash expresses a similar view: "Dearer to God than all of the Israelites who stood at Mount Sinai is the convert. Had the Israelites not witnessed the lightning, thunder, quaking mountain, and sounding trumpets they would not have accepted the Torah. But the convert, who did not see or hear any of these things, came and surrendered himself to God and took the yoke of heaven upon himself. Can anyone be dearer to God than such a person?" (Tanchuma Buber, Lech Lecha 6, 32).

What was the talmudic procedure for conversion?

The following is a description from the Talmud of the process of conversion:

> Our Rabbis taught: "Currently, if a person comes to a convert, he is addressed as follows: 'What have you seen that you came to be a proselyte; don't you know that Israel at the present time is persecuted and oppressed, despised, harassed, and overcome by afflictions?' If he replies: 'I know and yet am unworthy,' he is accepted immediately, and is given instruction in some of the minor and some of the major commandments ... He is also told of the punishment for the transgression of the commandments.. and he is informed of the reward granted for their fulfillment... He is not, however, persuaded or dissuaded too much. If he accepts the commandments, he is circumcised... As soon as he is healed, arrangements are made for his immediate immersion in a *mikvah*, where two learned men must stand by his side and acquaint him with some of the minor commandments and with some of the major ones. When he comes up after his immersion, he is deemed to be an Israelite in all respects." (Yevamot 47a)

This description above remains the basis for the traditional conversion even today. It is customary for a rabbi initially to discourage a prospective convert three times (because the Bible says "return" three times in the case of Ruth the Moabitess). If the person persists and is truly sincere, then he or she is offered the opportunity to learn about Judaism and have the rabbi as a sponsor.

What are the initial steps in the modern conversion process?

There is no uniform practice in Conservative Judaism with regard to the conversion process. There are, however, many common practices which are followed.

After a prospective candidate meets with a rabbi to discuss his or her situation, the rabbi will ask many questions in order to become better acquainted with the candidate's motives for conversion. The rabbi will likely want to determine some information related to family background and the degree of involvement of the candidate's present religion. Usually the candidate will not be accepted immediately. More often the candidate will be informed of the many difficulties that he or she might face as a Jew and the challenges and new responsibilities that would have to be assumed. The discussion might also include sociological findings about mixed marriages and the problems that are created here.

If the candidate persists after these discussions and the rabbi believes that the candidate has sincere and honest motives, then the rabbi will offer to sponsor the candidate and help see him or her through the conversion procedure.

There is no uniform prescription for the length of the conversion period and the training involved. It is quite likely that the candidate will be asked to participate in formal classes or private sessions with the rabbi, learning Hebrew, Jewish history, customs, and ceremonies and life cycle events.

This period of preparation may last from six months to a year or longer. In many large cities Conservative congregations may have their own conversion class, or even a conversion institute sponsored by the local Rabbinical Assembly. These schools generally consist of several faculty members interacting with the prospective convert. In addition, the convert's Jewish partner (if one exists) is also generally required to attend.

What are the details of the final steps leading to conversion?

When the rabbi is satisfied that the prospective convert is truly knowledgeable about Judaism and sincere about living a Jewish life, the final step is taken. Arrangements are made by the rabbi for the prospective convert to go before a *Bet Din*, a court of three Jews (often rabbis) . The court will convene at a place where there is a *mikvah*. If no *mikvah* exists in a particular community, the Rabbinical Assembly's Law Committee has said that a natural body of water or even a swimming pool is acceptable.

If the candidate is a male, he must be ritually circumcised before attending the appointment with the *Bet Din*. If he has already been circumcised, as is very common today, then he must undergo the *hatafat dam brit*, the symbolic circumcision, which consists of shedding a drop of blood. This is done by a *mohel* or *mohelet* or knowledgeable Jewish physician who recites these two special blessings:

בָּרוּךְ אַתָּה יְיָ אֱלֹהֵינוּ מֶלֶךְ הָעוֹלָם, אֲשֶׁר קִדְּשָׁנוּ בְּמִצְוֹתָיו וְצִוָּנוּ לָמוּל אֶת־הַגֵּרִים.

Baruch ata Adonai elohenu melech haolam asher kidshanu bemitzvotav vetzivanu lamul et hagerim.

Praised are You, Adonai, who has made us holy with *mitzvot* and commanded us to circumcise converts.

בָּרוּךְ אַתָּה יְיָ אֱלֹהֵינוּ מֶלֶךְ הָעוֹלָם, אֲשֶׁר קִדְּשָׁנוּ בְּמִצְוֹתָיו
וְצִוָּנוּ לָמוּל אֶת־הַגֵּרִים וּלְהַטִּיף מֵהֶם דַּם בְּרִית שֶׁאִלְמָלֵא
דַּם בְּרִית לֹא נִתְקַיְמוּ שָׁמַיִם וָאָרֶץ, שֶׁנֶּאֱמַר: אִם־לֹא
בְרִיתִי יוֹמָם וָלַיְלָה חֻקּוֹת שָׁמַיִם וָאָרֶץ לֹא־שַׂמְתִּי. בָּרוּךְ
אַתָּה יְיָ, כּוֹרֵת הַבְּרִית.

Praised are You, God, who has made us holy with
mitzvot and commanded us to circumcise the converts
and to shed a drop of blood from the blood of
the covenant. For were it not for the blood of the
covenant, heaven and earth would not exist. As it is
said: Were it not for My covenant daily and nightly,
the rules of heaven and earth I could not set. Praised
are You, God, Creator of the covenant.

Once arriving at the place of the *mikvah,* the members of the
Bet Din will first get to know the person by asking questions
about background and commitment to Jewish life. Other
questions, both of a factual nature (e. g., Why do Jews not
eat bread on Passover?) or opinion-related (e. g., What is
your favorite Jewish prayer and talk about its meaning.) are
asked by the *Bet Din.*

When the *Bet Din* decides that the person has "passed the
test," the candidate is then invited to immerse in the *mikvah.* The candidate disrobes, and with the witnesses waiting
outside at the door, the candidate immerses. Following the
immersion, the candidate recites these two blessings:

בָּרוּךְ אַתָּה יְיָ אֱלֹהֵינוּ מֶלֶךְ הָעוֹלָם, אֲשֶׁר קִדְּשָׁנוּ בְּמִצְוֹתָיו וְצִוָּנוּ
עַל הַטְּבִילָה.

*Baruch ata Adonai elohenu melech haolam asher kid-
shanu bemitzvotav vetzivanu al hatevilla.*

Praised are You, Adonai, who makes us holy with

mitzvot and commanded us concerning ritual immersion.

בָּרוּךְ אַתָּה יְיָ אֱלֹהֵינוּ מֶלֶךְ הָעוֹלָם שֶׁהֶחֱיָנוּ וְקִיְּמָנוּ
וְהִגִּיעָנוּ לַזְּמַן הַזֶּה:

*Baruch ata Adonai elohenu melech haolam she-
hecheeyanu vekeemanu veheegeeyanu lazman hazeh.*

Praised Are You. God, who has kept us in life and sustained us, and enabled us to reach this occasion.

After the immersion a short ceremony follows during which the document of conversion is signed by members of the *Bet Din.* Some rabbis will have the successful candidate recite a declaration of faith and the prayer *Shema Yisrael.* This may be followed with the rabbi officially welcoming the candidate into the community of Israel and conferring upon the candidate a Hebrew name. The Hebrew names of *Avraham* (Abraham) for a male convert or *Sarah* (Sara) and *Rute* (Ruth) for a female convert are popular choices. However, converts may choose any Hebrew name that they wish. It is customary for all converts to Judaism to be called the son or daughter of Abraham and Sarah, since they were our first Jewish patriarch and matriarch. After the conferring of the Hebrew name the rabbi may choose to offer this special *mi sheberach prayer:*

Male:

מִי שֶׁבֵּרַךְ אֲבוֹתֵינוּ אַבְרָהָם יִצְחָק וְיַעֲקֹב, הוּא יְבָרֵךְ אֶת־אָחִינוּ
בֶּן אַבְרָהָם אָבִינוּ בְּבוֹאוֹ לַחֲסוֹת תַּחַת כַּנְפֵי הַשְּׁכִינָה וּלְהִסְתַּפֵּחַ
בְּנַחֲלַת יִשְׂרָאֵל וּבְהִמָּנוֹתוֹ עַל גֵּרֵי הַצֶּדֶק בְּתוֹךְ עַם אֱלֹהֵי אַבְרָהָם.
יְהִי רָצוֹן שֶׁיַּצְלִיחַ בְּדַרְכּוֹ וְיִרְאֶה בְרָכָה בְּכָל־מַעֲשֵׂה יָדָיו, וְנֹאמַר
אָמֵן.

Female:

מִי שֶׁבֵּרַךְ אֲבוֹתֵינוּ אַבְרָהָם יִצְחָק וְיַעֲקֹב, שָׂרָה רִבְקָה רָחֵל וְלֵאָה
הוּא יְבָרֵךְ אֶת־אֲחוֹתֵנוּ בַּת אַבְרָהָם אָבִינוּ בְּבוֹאָה לַחֲסוֹת תַּחַת
כַּנְפֵי הַשְּׁכִינָה וּלְהִסְתַּפֵּחַ בְּנַחֲלַת יִשְׂרָאֵל וּבְהַמְנוֹתָהּ עַל גֵּרֵי
הַצֶּדֶק בְּתוֹךְ עַם אֱלֹהֵי אַבְרָהָם. יְהִי רָצוֹן שֶׁתַּצְלִיחַ בְּדַרְכָּהּ
וְתֵרָאֶה בְרָכָה בְּכָל־מַעֲשֵׂה יָדֶיהָ, וְנֹאמַר אָמֵן.

May God who blessed our ancestors, Abraham, Isaac
and Jacob (Sarah, Rebecca, Rachel and Leah), bless
_____. who has cast his (her) lot
with the people of Israel. He (she) is a true proselyte
among the people of the God of Abraham. May he
(she) prosper in all his (her) worthy endeavors; may
the work of his (her) hands be blessed. And let us
say: Amen.

The rabbi may choose to conclude with the three-fold
priestly blessing.

יְבָרֶכְךָ יְיָ וְיִשְׁמְרֶךָ,
יָאֵר יְיָ פָּנָיו אֵלֶיךָ וִיחֻנֶּךָּ.
יִשָּׂא יְיָ פָּנָיו אֵלֶיךָ וְיָשֵׂם לְךָ שָׁלוֹם.

May God bless you and keep you
May God's Presence shine and be good to you.
May God's face turn toward you and give you peace.

What is the process of conversion for a child?

There is one type of conversion that is unique, and that is
the conversion of a child. An adopted child whose biological
parents are known to be non-Jewish or a child born of
a non-Jewish woman will need to undergo conversion in
order to be considered a full participant in Judaism.

Conversion into Judaism must be voluntary. However, since children are not in a position to act on their own, non Jewish children are converted *al da'at bet din* (i.e., by the advice and consent of the Jewish court). This is permitted because it is deemed a privilege for a child to be converted to Judaism.

The conversion process for a child is the same as that for an adult. This means that boys must be ritually circumcised, and both boys and girls must be immersed in the *mikvah*. The conversion can be done at any age but will normally be postponed until the child is not afraid of the water.

Since the conversion of a child is not voluntary, a child does have the option of annulling it on the day he or she reaches the age of *bar* or *bat mitzvah*.

10

Adoption

He who raises an orphaned child is regarded by Torah as
if he had given birth to the child.

—Megillah 13a

HISTORICAL BACKGROUND

The history of adoption dates back to biblical times. Already in the Book of Exodus we learn that "Pharaoh's daughter said to her: 'Take this child [Moses] and nurse it for me, and I will give you your wages.' And the woman took the child and nursed it. And the child grew, and she brought him to Pharoah's daughter, and he became her son" (Exodus 2:9–10). In this early example Pharaoh's daughter "adopts" Moses as her own.

In the Book of Esther, we read the following: "And he brought up Hadassah, that is, Esther, his uncle's daughter; for she had neither father nor mother, and the maiden was of beautiful form and fair to look upon; and when her father and mother died, Mordecai took her for his own daughter' (Esther 2:7). Here we see that Esther is adopted by her cousin Mordecai.

Adoption today is defined as the legal proceeding whereby a person takes another person into the relation of a child and acquires the rights and responsibilities of a parent in respect of the other person. The institution of adoption is mentioned as far back in history as the Code of Hammurabi and reached its fullest development with the Romans. You might remember the well-known adoption of Octavian by Julius Caesar.

In modern times, adoption generally results from the desire of childless parents to raise a family.

What does Jewish tradition say about adoption?

In Jewish life, adoption resulting from the desire of a family that cannot have children to have them, is a recent phenomenon. The Bible does mention compassionate persons taking an orphan into their house (as Mordecai did with Esther), but we do not find the establishment of an artificial kinship that requires special court action.

There is no ancient Hebrew word for adoption and no mention of it in the standard codes of Jewish law. Traditionally, the adopted child in Judaism retained the status of its natural parent, and the adoptive parents were the legal guardians.

Today, the release of children for adoption is so rare that Jewish families are far more concerned with practices relating to the adoption of non-Jewish children.

What are some of the obligations of adoptive Jewish parents today?

The following are some of the Jewish legal stipulations that adoptive parents will need to think about before adopting a child:

1. If the biological mother of the child is not Jewish, the child will need to undergo the conversion as described in the conversion section of this book.
2. If the child is of unknown parentage, it is to be assumed that the parents are Gentile.
3. Theoretically, if the natural parents are Jewish, the adopted child should bear his natural father's name when using the patronymic "son of so and so"; if the natural parents are not Jewish, and the child is converted, it would be given the name of "so and so" [Hebrew] ben Avraham. It is however, permitted to use the Hebrew name of the adoptive father.
4. If the adopted child's natural father is Jewish, the child would take on the same status of his natural father. For example, if his nature father was a *kohen*, he would also be a *kohen*.

5. In the areas of the obligations of adoptive parents in matters of inheritance, maintenance, and the like, the law to be followed here would be the civil law of the land.

What are the components of a Jewish adoption ceremony?

The following is a simple Covenant of Adoption ceremony for a child named Noah Chanan.

בָּרוּךְ הַבָּא בְּשֵׁם יְיָ.

Baruch haba beshem Adonai.

May you be blessed in the name of God.

Noah is escorted into the room by his grandmothers. The parents of Noah explain the nature of the adoption ceremony and the significance of the baby's name. Verses from Psalm 119, the initial letters spelling out Noah Chanan in Hebrew, are recited in Hebrew and English by friends and family. (Note: Psalm 119 is an alphabetical acrostic whose many verses can be used in many creative ways, particularly in spelling out the names of persons)

נֵר־לְרַגְלִי דְבָרֶךָ וְאוֹר לִנְתִיבָתִי:

Your word is a lamp to my feet, a light for my path.

חֲצוֹת־לַיְלָה אָקוּם לְהוֹדוֹת לָךְ עַל מִשְׁפְּטֵי צִדְקֶךָ:

Arise at midnight—to praise You for Your just rules.

חָבֵר אָנִי לְכָל־אֲשֶׁר יְרֵאוּךָ וּלְשֹׁמְרֵי פִּקוּדֶיךָ:

I am a friend to all who stand in awe of You, to those who keep Your precepts.

נִדְבוֹת פִּי רְצֵה־נָא יְיָ וּמִשְׁפָּטֶיךָ לַמְּדֵנִי:

Accept, O God, the gifts of my mouth; teach me Your
ways.

נָחַלְתִּי עֵדְוֹתֶיךָ לְעוֹלָם כִּי־שְׂשׂוֹן לִבִּי הֵמָּה:

Your decrees are my eternal heritage; they are my
heart's delight.

Noah is placed on the knees of his adoptive parents. They
take an oath to raise the child as their own in accordance
with Jewish tradition and values:

נִשְׁבָּעִים אֲנַחְנוּ בְּשֵׁם מִי שֶׁשְּׁמוֹ רַחוּם וְחַנּוּן שֶׁנְּקַיֵּים
אֶת הַיֶּלֶד/הַיַּלְדָּה הַזֶּה/הַזֹּאת כְּאִילוּ הָיָה/הָיְתָה מִזַּרְעֵנוּ
יוֹצֵא/יוֹצֵאת חֲלָצֵנוּ. וּנְגַדְּלוֹ/וּנְגַדְּלָה וְנַחֲזִיקוֹ/וְנַחֲזִיקָה
וְנַדְרִיכוֹ/וְנַדְרִיכָה בְּדַרְכֵּי תּוֹרָתֵנוּ, כְּכָל מִצְווֹת הַבֵּן/הַבַּת עַל
הָאָב וְהָאֵם. יְהִי ה' אֱלֹהֵינוּ עִמּוֹ/עִמָּה בְּכֹל מַעֲשֵׂה יָדָיו/יָדֶיהָ.
אָמֵן כֵּן יְהִי רָצוֹן.

*Nishba'im anahnu besheim mi sheshemo rahum vehanun
shnekayeim et hayeled hazeh ke'ilu haya mizar'einu yot-
sei halatseinu. Unegadeleinu venahzikeinu venadrikheinu
bedarkheinu bedarkhei torateinu kekhol mitsvot habein al
ha'av veha'eim. Yehi Adonai elohav immo bekhol ma'asei
yadav, Amein, kein yehi ratson.*

We solemnly swear, by God who is called loving and
merciful, that we will raise this child as our own.
We will nurture him, sustain him, and guide him in
the paths of Torah, in accordance with the duties
incumbent upon Jewish parents. May God ever be
with him. We pray for the wisdom and strength to
help our child Noah become a man of integrity.

הַמַּלְאָךְ הַגֹּאֵל אֹתִי מִכָּל־רָע יְבָרֵךְ אֶת־הַנְּעָרִים וְיִקָּרֵא
בָהֶם שְׁמִי וְשֵׁם אֲבֹתַי אַבְרָהָם וְיִצְחָק וְיִדְגּוּ לָרֹב בְּקֶרֶב
הָאָרֶץ:

May the One who saved me from all evil, bless these
children, and let them be called by our name and
the names of our ancestors and may they multiply
throughout the land.

The Blessing of Peace:

יְבָרֶכְךָ יְיָ וְיִשְׁמְרֶךָ,

May God bless you and guard you.

יָאֵר יְיָ פָּנָיו אֵלֶיךָ וִיחֻנֶּךָּ,

May God illuminate you with light and show you
grace.

יִשָּׂא יְיָ פָּנָיו אֵלֶיךָ וְיָשֵׂם לְךָ שָׁלוֹם.

May God's face turn towards you and grant you peace.

Everyone joins in reciting the *shehecheeyanu*.

בָּרוּךְ אַתָּה יְיָ אֱלֹהֵינוּ מֶלֶךְ הָעוֹלָם שֶׁהֶחֱיָנוּ וְקִיְּמָנוּ וְהִגִּיעָנוּ לַזְּמַן
הַזֶּה:

*Baruch ata Adonai elohenu melech haolam shehecheeyanu
vekeemanu veheegeeyanu lazman hazeh.*

Praised are You, God, who has kept us in life and
sustained us and enabled us to reach this occasion.

This is followed by the blessings over the wine and the bread.

בָּרוּךְ אַתָּה יְיָ אֱלֹהֵינוּ מֶלֶךְ הָעוֹלָם, בּוֹרֵא פְּרִי הַגָּפֶן.

Baruch ata Adonai elohenu melech ha'olam boray pri hagafen.

Praised are You God who creates the fruit of the vine.

בָּרוּךְ אַתָּה יְיָ אֱלֹהֵינוּ מֶלֶךְ הָעוֹלָם, הַמּוֹצִיא לֶחֶם מִן הָאָרֶץ:

Baruch ata Adonai elohenu melech ha'olam hamotzi lechem min ha'aretz.

Praised are You Adonai who brings forth bread from the earth.

11

Death and Mourning

The dust returns to the earth as it was, but the spirit returns to God who gave it.

—Ecclesiastes 3:2

What does Jewish tradition say about death and dying?

Just as there is a Jewish way of life, so too there is a Jewish way of death. Over the centuries the rabbis have designed a pattern of practices and rituals which are concerned with every aspect of death. These laws and practices are based upon two fundamental principles:

1. The honor and respect due even to a lifeless human being. In Hebrew this concept is known as *kevod hamet* ("respecting the deceased").
2. The concern for the mental, emotional and spiritual well being of the living mourners, and the requirement of extending comfort to them. In Hebrew we call this concept *nichum avelim* ("comforting the mourners").

In America today, the dying are often isolated in hospitals and find themselves alone and often unable to cope with the reality of their illness. Our society tends to deny death, and many people opt to avoid those whose death is imminent, not knowing what to say or do for such persons.

The Jewish way of death is one that emphasizes both honesty and realism. Centuries ago, King David honestly faced his own death: "Behold, I am now about to go in the way of all the earth," he said to his son Solomon. It is as simple and undeniable as that. There are several underlying Jewish themes which relate to the Jewish way of death. They are:

1. **Reality:** Judaism views death realistically. Death is a part of life, and it is important to face it with extreme honesty. For example, the plain white robe (called a *kittel*) that traditional Jews wear on the Day of Atonement and at the Passover seder, is both the garment of freedom and the traditional burial shroud. The custom of having the

mourner help bury the dead by shoveling earth into the grave is yet another example of Judaism's realistic view of death.

2. **Simplicity:** Simplicity and modesty constitute another well-known motif that pervades the entire Jewish tradition. With regard to death, the prescription for a simple wooden coffin is meant to avoid ostentation and excessive cost and is a reminder of the democracy of death. In the eyes of God, all are equal, whatever their social status may be.

3. **Community:** When we lose a loved one, it is especially comforting to know that we can expect the customary outreach of the Jewish community and thus know that we are never alone. As an act of kindness, the mourner's first meal after the burial is prepared by others. The congregation moves into the mourner's home and services will usually be held there during the week of mourning.

The psychological insight of Jewish wisdom is nowhere more evident than in the manner in which it addresses death and mourning. All of the rituals surrounding death and mourning directly address themselves to maintaining the dignity of the deceased and to comforting the pain of the mourners.

BEFORE DEATH

What is the mitzvah of visiting the sick?

It is a great *mitzvah* in Judaism to visit the sick, which in Hebrew is called *bikkur cholim*. The rabbis designated visiting the sick as an important act of lovingkindness which is so important that it is numbered among those things for which a person enjoys the fruits in this world, while the principal reward is held for him in the world-to-come (Shabbat 127a).

Societies for visiting the sick were prevalent in many European Jewish communities. Societies for visiting the sick were also founded by Jewish immigrants in America, and there are a number of Conservative congregations that have their own societies.

There are several important rabbinic guidelines for the practice of visiting the sick. For instance, it is important that one's visits be made at appropriate times and not last too long. Lengthy visits will often make the patient fatigued and uncomfortable. One should also not visit the sick immediately after they have fallen ill, lest they become frightened. Most importantly, the rabbis always wanted the visitors to remember that the primary purpose of their visitation was to make the patient comfortable and cheer him or her up.

Does Judaism have a ritual of confession?

Judaism does have a confessional prayer which is intended to help put one's spiritual house in order. In it one asks forgiveness for one's sins which is followed by a confirming statement of faith in God (*Shema Yisrael*). The confession prayer, known as the *vidui*, may be recited for a very ill person when that person is unable to do so. The following is one version of the *vidui*:

> I acknowledge before You, Adonai, that my life and death are in Your hands. May it be Your Will to heal me. But, if death is my fate, then I accept it from Your hand with love. O God, bestow upon me the abounding happiness that is stored for righteous people. Make known to me the path of life. In Your Presence is fullness of joy. At Your right hand is eternal bliss. Protect my family. Into Your hands I offer my spirit. You have redeemed me, God of truth. Amen.

What is an ethical will?

When Jacob felt that he was close to death, he asked for divine mercy, saying, "May it please You to grant that a person shall fall ill for two or three days and then be gathered into our people, in order that he may have time to put his house in order and repent of his sins." God replied, "It shall be so and you shall be the first to profit from this opportunity."

Jacob's blessing to his children (Genesis 49) established a custom that gained popularity during the Middle Ages. Parents and grandparents, before their deaths, often wrote letters and messages to their children in which they expressed their hopes and wishes for their children and the values which they hoped would be continued by them.

Today there are parents and grandparents who have reinstated the custom of writing an ethical will to their children, thus providing their families with an important spiritual legacy.

FROM DEATH TO BEREAVEMENT

What is an onen?

In Jewish practice, the first stage or phase of the mourning process is called *aninut*. It begins when a person learns of the death of an immediate relative and ends when the interment or burial takes place. A person who has lost a relative and is going through *aninut* is called an *onen*. Because the initial shock when learning of a loved one can be traumatic, Jewish law exempts the *onen* from the performance of all positive religious obligations, such as reciting the evening and morning prayers. The reason for this prescription is twofold. First, since the bereaved is obligated to attend to the needs of the deceased, there should be nothing to distract him from these obligations. Second, it is considered a breach of the principle of honoring the deceased to do anything but attend to the deceased.

What does one do when death first occurs?

When death finally does come, the eyes and mouth of the deceased should be closed and the body covered with a sheet. This is an act of respect to the departed. Then those present may recite the traditional phrase *Baruch dayan ha'emet,* "Praised be the Righteous Judge."

Next, one would customarily call one's rabbi who in turn would likely notify the *chevra kaddisha* (burial society) should there be one in the community. The rabbi would also call the funeral home to make arrangements for the transfer of the deceased, for the funeral, and for the burial. The rabbi would also help to set the time and date for the funeral.

The custom has been to have a watchperson (*shomer*) stay with the deceased from the time of death until the burial. When a death occurs in a hospital, some of these rituals are delayed unto the deceased is moved to the funeral home.

What is the chevra kaddisha?

Chevra kaddisha literally means "holy society" and refers to those individuals in a community whose responsibility it is to care for the body and prepare it in strict accordance with Jewish law for burial. This society originated several centuries ago and was part of a communal system for assuring that the deceased be properly cared for. In some modern synagogues today, the *chevra kaddisha* is called the "caring committee."

What does the chevra kaddisha do?

The *chevra kaddisha* cares for the body of the deceased

from death until burial. Its members perform a series of highly ritualized acts known as a *tahara*, "purification" of the body. The procedure generally takes place in a special room in the funeral home. All parts of the deceased's body are washed in a strict and prescribed sequence while prayers and psalms are recited. *Tachrichim* (shrouds) of white linen or cotton cloth are placed on the body. White is a sign of purity, and the shrouds are all alike to remind us that in death, all are equal. A deceased male (and any female whose family elects to do so) is wrapped in a *tallit* (prayer shawl), with one *tzitzit* (fringe) cut, symbolizing that one who has died is no longer responsible to observe the *mitzvot* ("religious commandments").

A bag of earth from Israel is customarily placed into the casket and often sprinkled upon the deceased. Symbolically, at least, the deceased is being buried in the soil of the Holy Land.

What kind of casket must be used?

In ancient Palestine, the dead were often wrapped in cloth and placed into the niches of caves. Abraham, for example, was buried in the Cave of Machpelah. Use of actual caskets dates from the period of the Babylonian exile, and by about the seventeenth century, Eastern European Jews had complete solid caskets.

In accordance with the Jewish concept of equality of all persons in death, simplicity is the keynote of the day. Conservative Judaism prescribes the use of a coffin that is made entirely of wood. Such a casket conforms well with the biblical passage "You are dust and unto dust shall you return" (Genesis 3:19). The plain pine casket is the most traditional and least ostentatious, and it is a popular choice among traditional Conservative Jews.

Can people "view" the deceased after the tahara?

Contrary to the practice in many communities, honor to the deceased, according to Jewish tradition, dictates that viewing of the body is highly improper and disrespectful. Although there have been psychotherapists who have lauded the therapeutic value inherent in the practice of viewing, this has never been proven clinically. Viewing the corpse is objectionable, both theologically and psychologically. A human being, created in the image of God, participating in the dignity of human life, deserves to rest in peace. And the mourner deserves, at this traumatic moment of intense grief, to be allowed to work through, naturally and at his or her own pace, an acknowledgment and acceptance of the loss. It is much more important to remember how the individual looked in life than in death.

When does a Jewish funeral take place?

Traditionally, funerals take place within twenty-four hours of death, according to the guiding principle of honoring the dead. A delay in burial is permitted only if it is for purposes of honoring the dead, as it would be if the delay was to provide time to procure the shrouds and coffin or to await the arrival of important out-of-town relatives. Postponement is required when "within twenty four hours" would mean that burial would take place on Shabbat or a Jewish holiday, which is not permitted. Convenience, itself, is no reason to delay a funeral.

Although embalming of a body is expressly forbidden by Jewish law, it is allowed when a lengthy delay in the funeral service seems mandatory and when a burial takes place overseas, such as in Israel.

Where may a Jewish funeral take place?

Historically, Jewish funerals took place at the home of the deceased or at the cemetery. Synagogues were not used, unless the deceased was a person of extraordinary distinction or stature in the community.

Today, some communities permit funeral services to be held in the synagogue. In others, the funeral home is the rule. They are generally designed to accommodate large numbers of people and their professional expertise affords a dignified funeral.

Can children attend the funeral?

Children need to be provided with the opportunity to grieve in their own way. Children certainly may attend funerals, and those who want to attend should be permitted to do so. One's family rabbi will often sit down with the family, including the children, prior to the funeral. The rabbi will explain what will take place during the funeral, often alleviating any fears or concerns that may be on the minds of the children.

Should flowers be sent to the funeral parlor?

Sephardic custom allows for flowers, and there is no real prohibition against using them in Ashkenazi practice. Well-wishers, though, ought to be encouraged to give *tzedakah* (charity) in memory of the deceased. This custom began in the Middle Ages and to this day has been a more authentic way of showing honor to the deceased and comfort to the bereaved.

Who is a mourner?

According to Jewish tradition, one is required to observe the laws of mourning for these seven relatives: father, mother, spouse, son, daughter, sister, and brother.

THE FUNERAL AND THE BURIAL

What is keriah?

The Hebrew word *keriah* means "rending" or "tearing" of the clothing. In biblical times it was customary to cut one's garment upon hearing the sad news of the loss of a loved one. The present law requires *keriah* only for those relatives for whom one must observe the mourning period. (the seven relatives just cited). The rending is an opportunity for psychological relief, allowing the mourner to express anguish and vent one's feelings.

The *keriah* is the tear made on the mourner's clothing (or on a ribbon attached to the clothing) as an outward sign of grief. It is usually done immediately before the funeral service. For a deceased parent, *keriah* is customarily on the left side, closest to the heart. For all others, *keriah* is on the right side. Immediately prior to *keriah* the following benediction is recited by the mourner:

בָּרוּךְ אַתָּה יְיָ אֱלֹהֵינוּ מֶלֶךְ הָעוֹלָם, דַּיַּן הָאֱמֶת.

Baruch ata Adonai elohenu melech haolam dayan ha'emet.

Praised are You, Adonai our God, You are the true Judge.

Much like the Mourner's Kaddish, this prayer is a reaffirmation of faith in God in time of great sorrow.

What happens at the funeral?

The Hebrew word for funeral is *levayah,* which literally means "accompaniment." Jewish funerals require community involvement. It is a *mitzvah* to attend the funeral and to accompany the deceased to the cemetery. Pallbearers, or "honorary" pallbearers, generally carry the casket or walk beside the coffin from the chapel to the hearse, and, at times, also from the hearse to the grave itself. Members of the family or close friends are often honored as the pallbearers.

A very simple service is prescribed by Jewish law for the funeral itself. There is no standard or fixed funeral service, so variations abound. However, there are a number of elements that most funerals do have in common.

Generally speaking, the officiating rabbi will read a selection or two from the book of Psalms, deliver a eulogy, and chant the memorial prayer *El Malei Rachamim* at the service's conclusion.

It is important for the family of the deceased to provide the substance for the eulogy. Abraham, our first patriarch, eulogized his wife Sarah. Family members ought to be encouraged to speak at the funeral, if they are emotionally able to do so. In their doing so they not only pay honor to the memory of their loved one but bring comfort to their family and friends who are present.

The recessional, performed by wheeling or carrying the casket from the funeral chapel or synagogue to the hearse, is often led by the rabbi, who recites psalms.

What happens at the cemetery?

Upon arriving at the cemetery, pallbearers (if the cemetery rules permit) carry the casket to the grave. This custom dates back to bible times, when Jacob's children carried him to his grave. Seven stops are customarily made by the pallbearers on their way to the grave, symbolizing the seven times that the word "vanity" occurs in the Book of Ecclesiastes. Others assert that each of the seven pauses symbolizes one of the seven heavens of mystical lore.

A prayer called *tzidduk hadin,* which is an acceptance of

God's judgment, is usually recited at the graveside. Its words
begin: "The Rock, God's work is perfect, for all God's ways
are judgment..."

A few closing words are then said by the rabbi, followed
by the lowering of the casket into the grave. This is usually
followed by the reciting of *El Malei Rachamim,* a prayer for
the peace of the departed soul. The reciting of the Mourner's
Kaddish closes the service.

For male:

אֵל מָלֵא רַחֲמִים, שׁוֹכֵן בַּמְּרוֹמִים, הַמְצֵא מְנוּחָה נְכוֹנָה תַּחַת כַּנְפֵי
הַשְּׁכִינָה, בְּמַעֲלוֹת קְדוֹשִׁים וּטְהוֹרִים כְּזֹהַר הָרָקִיעַ מַזְהִירִים, אֶת
נִשְׁמַת ____ בֶּן ____ שֶׁהָלַךְ לְעוֹלָמוֹ, אָנָּא, בַּעַל הָרַחֲמִים הַסְתִּירָהוּ
בְּסֵתֶר כְּנָפֶיךָ לְעוֹלָמִים, וּצְרוֹר בִּצְרוֹר הַחַיִּים אֶת־נִשְׁמָתוֹ, יְיָ הוּא
נַחֲלָתוֹ, וְיָנוּחַ בְּשָׁלוֹם עַל מִשְׁכָּבוֹ, וְנֹאמַר אָמֵן.

*El malei rachamim sho-chein bam'romim, hamm-tzei
m'nuchah n'khonah tahat kanfei ha-shechinah, b'ma-alot
k'doshim u-t'horim k'zohar ha-rakiya maz-hirim et nish-
mat ____ ben ____ sheh-halach le'olamo, b'gan eiden t'hei
menuchato. Ana, ba-al ha-rachamim, hassti-rei-hu b'seiter
k'nafecha l'olamim, u-tzror bi-tzror hachayim et nishmato,
Adonai hu nachalato, v'yanu'ach b'shalom al mishkavo,
v'nomar amen.*

Compassionate God, grant eternal peace in Your
protective Presence, among the holy and pure to the
soul of ___ who has returned to his eternal home.
Merciful One, remember his worthy deeds. May his
soul be given eternal life and may his memory inspire
us to be good people. And let us say: Amen.

For female:

אֵל מָלֵא רַחֲמִים שׁוֹכֵן בַּמְּרוֹמִים, הַמְצֵא מְנוּחָה נְכוֹנָה תַּחַת כַּנְפֵי הַשְּׁכִינָה, בְּמַעֲלוֹת קְדוֹשִׁים וּטְהוֹרִים כְּזֹהַר הָרָקִיעַ מַזְהִירִים, אֶת נִשְׁמַת ____ בַּת ____ שֶׁהָלְכָה לְעוֹלָמָהּ, בְּגַן עֵדֶן תְּהֵא מְנוּחָתָהּ. אָנָּא, בַּעַל הָרַחֲמִים הַסְתִּירֶהָ בְּסֵתֶר כְּנָפֶיךָ לְעוֹלָמִים, וּצְרוֹר בִּצְרוֹר הַחַיִּים אֶת נִשְׁמָתָהּ, יְיָ הוּא נַחֲלָתָהּ, וְתָנוּחַ בְּשָׁלוֹם עַל מִשְׁכָּבָהּ, וְנֹאמַר אָמֵן.

El malei rachamim sho-chein bam'romim, hamm-tzei m'nuchah n'khonah tahat kanfei ha-shechinah, b'ma-alot k'doshim u-t'horim k'zohar ha-rakiya maz-hirim et nish-mat ____ bat ____ sheh-halchah le'olamah, b'gan eiden t'hei menuchata. Ana, ba-al ha-rachamim, hassti-re-ha b'seiter k'nafecha l'olamim, u-tzror bi-tzror hachayim et nishmatah, Adonai hu nachalatah, v'tanu'ach b'shalom al mishkavah, v'nomar amen.

Compassionate God, grant eternal peace in Your protective Presence, among the holy and pure to the soul of ___ who has returned to her eternal home. Merciful One, remember her worthy deeds. May her soul be given eternal life and may her memory inspire us to be good people. And let us say: Amen.

The reciting of the Mourner's Kaddish closes the service.

Mourners:

יִתְגַּדַּל וְיִתְקַדַּשׁ שְׁמֵהּ רַבָּא בְּעָלְמָא דִּי בְרָא כִרְעוּתֵהּ וְיַמְלִיךְ מַלְכוּתֵהּ בְּחַיֵּיכוֹן וּבְיוֹמֵיכוֹן וּבְחַיֵּי דְכָל בֵּית יִשְׂרָאֵל בַּעֲגָלָא וּבִזְמַן קָרִיב וְאָמְרוּ אָמֵן:

Yitgadal veyitkadash shmey raba
B'alma divra chirutei veyamlich malchutei
Bechayechon uveyamechon uvchayeh dechol beyt yisrael
Baagala uvizman kariv vimru amen

Cong. and Mourners:

יְהֵא שְׁמֵהּ רַבָּא מְבָרַךְ לְעָלַם וּלְעָלְמֵי עָלְמַיָּא:

Yehey shmey raba mevarach l'alam ulalmey almaya

Mourners:

יִתְבָּרַךְ וְיִשְׁתַּבַּח וְיִתְפָּאַר וְיִתְרוֹמַם וְיִתְנַשֵּׂא וְיִתְהַדָּר וְיִתְעַלֶּה
וְיִתְהַלָּל שְׁמֵהּ דְּקוּדְשָׁא, בְּרִיךְ הוּא. לְעֵלָּא (וּלְעֵלָּא) מִן כָּל
בִּרְכָתָא וְשִׁירָתָא תֻּשְׁבְּחָתָא וְנֶחֱמָתָא דַּאֲמִירָן בְּעָלְמָא וְאִמְרוּ
אָמֵן:

*Yitbarach veyishtabach vyitpaar veyitromom veyitnasey
Veyithadar veyitaleh veyithalal shmey dekudsha brich hu,
Leyla (uleyla) min kol birchata veshirata tushbechata
vnechemata daamiran bealma vimru amen*

Mourners:

יְהֵא שְׁלָמָא רַבָּא מִן־שְׁמַיָּא וְחַיִּים עָלֵינוּ וְעַל־כָּל־יִשְׂרָאֵל. וְאִמְרוּ
אָמֵן:

*Yehey shlama raba min shemaya Vechayim aleynu ve'al
kol yisrael vimru amen*

Mourners:

עוֹשֶׂה שָׁלוֹם בִּמְרוֹמָיו הוּא יַעֲשֶׂה שָׁלוֹם עָלֵינוּ וְעַל־כָּל־יִשְׂרָאֵל.
וְאִמְרוּ אָמֵן:

*Oseh shalom bimromav hu yaaseh shalom aleynu ve'al kol
yisrael vimru amen.*

Magnified and sanctified be the name of God
throughout the world which God has created according to God's will. May God establish a kingdom
during the days of your life and during the life of
all the House of Israel, speedily, soon; and say you,
Amen.

all the House of Israel, speedily, soon; and say you, Amen.

Congregation and Mourners

May God's great name be blessed for ever and ever.

Mourners

Exalted and honored be the name of the Holy One, blessed be God, whose glory transcends, and is beyond all praises, hymns and blessings that people can render to God; and say you, Amen.

May there be abundant peace from heaven, and life for us and for all Israel: and say you, Amen.

May God who establishes peace in the heavens, grant peace unto us and unto all Israel; and say you, Amen.

It is a *mitzvah* in Judaism to bury the dead. This is accomplished by relatives and friends of the family shoveling the earth back into the grave to cover the casket. Often, as difficult as this is to do, it is the last physical act of love that can be performed to honor the deceased, and it helps the mourners on the way to acceptance and reconciliation.

After the casket is covered, those present are asked to form two parallel lines, facing each other. As the rabbi asks the mourners to pass through the two lines, those present recite these traditional words of comfort:

הַמָּקוֹם יְנַחֵם אֶתְכֶם בְּתוֹךְ שְׁאָר אֲבֵלֵי צִיוֹן וִירוּשָׁלָיִם.

Hamakom yenachem etchem betoch she'ar avelei tziyon verushalayim.

May God comfort you among the mourners for Zion and Jerusalem.

MOURNING OBSERVANCES

What is shiva?

Shiva, taken from the Hebrew word for seven, refers to the first seven days of mourning. The Talmud (Sanhedrin 108b) holds that the practice of a mourning period of seven days originated prior to the Flood, which is described in the story of Noah. The talmudic rabbis cite Genesis 7:10 as the earliest instance of *shiva*: "And it came to pass, after the seven days, that the waters of the flood were upon the earth." The seven days, the rabbis explain, were a period of mourning for Methuselah, the oldest person ever to have lived.

When does shiva begin?

Shiva begins immediately after the burial and concludes a short time after the morning service seven days later. The day of the interment is considered the first full day of mourning regardless of whether it included a full twenty-four hours or not. When a death occurs on the first day of a major festival (Passover, Shavuot, or Sukkot), the beginning of *shiva* is delayed until the end of the festival. Moreover, the onset of a major festival brings any *shiva* period to an end, regardless of how many days have elapsed.

What does a mourner do during shiva?

Shiva should be held in the home of the deceased. This allows the family to be together. Where this is not possible, *shiva* may be observed in the home of an immediate family member or even a friend.

It is customary for the mourner to refrain from work during *shiva.* Among some Jews, shaving (or haircutting of any sort) is avoided, as is personal grooming, except of course for hygienic purposes. New clothes are not to be worn and there is a prohibition against conjugal relations.

Certain *shiva* practices are things to be done immediately upon returning from the burial at the cemetery. First, one washes the hands. This is an ancient custom designed to cleanse oneself from the ritual impurity associated with death and the cemetery. Second, the mourners eat a meal of condolence, prepared in advance by their friends, as an affirmation of life. This enables and encourages a mourner to eat food, which he might otherwise not wish to do. The traditional food at the meal of condolence usually includes lentils, hard-boiled eggs, and bread, all foods which in Judaism are associated with life. Eggs in particular are a symbol of life and renewal.

During *shiva,* friends and members of the community will visit the mourners to formally express their condolences. It is customary to wait to speak until after the mourner speaks. The very presence of the friends and relatives of the mourner can be a true comfort and is often the greatest gift one can give a mourner.

What is the purpose of the shiva candle?

Upon arriving home, the mourner should light a candle that burns for seven days. This so called *shiva* candle is usually provided by the Jewish funeral director. It has been said that the candle represents the soul of the departed. Just as the candle sheds light, so the deceased brought light into the household. One candle is sufficient for the entire household. If, however, relatives are observing *shiva* in several homes, then it would be proper to light a candle in each of these homes.

Why are mirrors covered in a house of shiva?

While the covering of mirrors in the house of *shiva* has been customary for a long time, the reason for the custom is obscure. One possible reason is that a mirror is often seen as a sign of human vanity, and therefore is out of place at a house of mourning. Certainly a mourner should not be concerned with physical appearance and with the frills of life at a time such as this.

Why do mourners often refrain from wearing leather shoes and why do they sit on low stools?

It is customary to wear slippers or rubber or canvas shoes during *shiva*. The Talmud has stated that leather is a symbol of luxury. During *shiva* it is also the custom for mourners to sit lower than others, usually on low stools. Perhaps this is the origin of the expression "sitting" *shiva*. No one knows exactly how the custom of sitting lower originated. Some scholars cite Job 2:13 which describes Job's three friends coming to comfort him: "For seven days and seven nights they sat beside him on the ground."

May mourners leave their homes during shiva?

The mourners should stay at home during the seven days of *shiva*. Services will often be conducted by the rabbi, cantor, or congregational volunteers in the home where *shiva* is being observed. If a mourner is a person of modest means and must work in order to sustain himself, he is permitted to return to work on the third day of *shiva*. In addition, if a service cannot be arranged at the house of *shiva*, the mourners are permitted to go to synagogue for services and to say the Mourner's Kaddish. Finally, mourners are permitted to attend Sabbath services at the synagogue, but should not accept an *aliyah* to the Torah.

What happens at the conclusion of shiva?

When mourners arise from shiva on the seventh day, they customarily take a short walk, usually around the block, to symbolize their return to society. The mourners now enter the second phase of mourning, called *sheloshim*. As its Hebrew name indicates, this is a period of thirty days, reckoned from interment to include the seven days of *shiva*. *Sheloshim* customs begin on the morning of the seventh day of *shiva*. The twenty-three days following *shiva* are considerably less restrictive than the *shiva* itself. One may return to work and may return to marital relations. One usually avoids certain forms of entertainment and continues to say the Mourner's Kaddish in the context of the daily *minyan*. Technically, *sheloshim* ends the full mourning period for all relatives except for those grieving for their parents (whose length of mourning is a full year). In most communities, Kaddish for parents is said for only eleven months. Festivals also affect the observance of *sheloshim,* and it is best to consult with a rabbi for the exact details.

POSTMOURNING OBSERVANCES

How do we mourn after shiva is completed?

Mourning lasts a full year when one loses a parent. In a Hebrew leap year of thirteen months, mourning is required only for twelve months. Due to the principle of social visibility, the most stringent mourning restrictions, such as those in the area of personal grooming, are relaxed, because of the mourner's need to interact throughout the year with other people. Parties and social occasions are usually avoided, while Torah study and acts of *tzedakah* are to be encouraged.

What is the Kaddish prayer?

Kaddish is an Aramaic word meaning "sanctification." The Kaddish prayer itself is among the best known and most frequently recited Jewish prayers. There are many interesting theories related to the origin of the Kaddish prayer. Some scholars believe that it was written by Jews during the Babylonian Exile (586–538 B.C.E.) or by the rabbis of the first and second centuries C.E.

Interestingly, the Kaddish was not originally intended as a prayer for mourners. It was composed for recitation at the conclusion of a lesson in the house of study. Gradually it passed into the synagogue and then into the house of mourning. And so, although it is called the mourner's prayer, it does not include a single reference to death. Rather, it is an affirmation of faith in God. From its beginning to its end, the Kaddish sanctifies the name of God and attests to the mourner's total submission to, and acceptance of, God's will.

There are many forms of the prayer, one of which is the burial Kaddish and the other the Mourner's Kaddish. The burial Kaddish includes a paragraph about the eventual resurrection of the dead during the time of the Messiah. It is said only at the graveside. The Mourner's Kaddish is said throughout the year whenever the mourner is in the synagogue. Many rabbis will also use the Mourner's Kaddish at the cemetery.

Who says Kaddish, for whom is it recited and for how long?

Jewish law requires the recitation of the Mourner's Kaddish for parents, spouses, siblings, and children. For parents, Kaddish is generally to be recited for eleven months following burial. A passage in the Shulchan Aruch states that the maximum twelve month purification process of a soul was only required for totally evil persons. Since no mourner should ever acknowledge the possibility of completely wicked parents, the law shortened the required period to eleven months. For all other relatives, the Mourner's Kaddish is recited for thirty days, the period known as *sheloshim.*

Traditionally, the son is required to say the Mourner's Kaddish for deceased parents. Since this was such a respected *mitzvah,* parents would often refer to their sons as "my Kaddish." Conservative Judaism today has come to view this obligation as binding on daughters as well. These responsibilities ought not be transferred to another person.

What are the laws relating to the tombstone?

The use of tombstones is an ancient custom, dating back to biblical times. In the Book of Genesis (35:20), Jacob sets up a pillar at the site of his wife Rachel's grave. King Josiah saw the tombstone of a prophet and instructed that it not be disturbed. By the fifth or sixth centuries C.E., most Jewish burials involved tombstones, and by the the time of the *Shulchan Aruch* (sixteenth century), the custom had become binding law.

What are some guidelines for tombstone inscriptions?

Over the years, certain elements have become common for tombstones and markers in North America. The name of the deceased in English, and often in Hebrew, appears on the tombstone, along with the date of death according to both the secular and the Hebrew calendar. Sometimes above this inscription, among Ashkenazim, one finds the two Hebrew letters פ״נ, which is the abbreviation for *po nach*—"here rests." The Sephardim often use the Hebrew letters מ״ק standing for מַצֶּבֶת קְבוּרָה (*matzevet kevurah*), meaning "monument of the grave of . . . " Underneath the inscription one usually finds the Hebrew letters ת׳נ׳צ׳ב׳ה standing for תְּהִי נִשְׁמָתוֹ צְרוּרָה בִּצְרוֹר הַחַיִּים (*Tehi nishmato tzerurah bitzeror hachayim*), "May his soul be bound up on the bond of eternal life."

There are a number of pictorial symbols that also appear on tombstones. The seven-branched menorah, symbol of the Israelites in the Bible, is a common one. For Levites, a ewer, symbolizing the ancient cup of the Levites that was used to wash the priest's hands is often used. The tombstones of *kohanim,* the descendants of the ancient priests, will often be marked by the carving of raised hands for the Priestly Blessing. Occasionally there will be a verse from the Bible or some rabbinic text that relates in some fashion to the life of the deceased. For example, Proverbs 31 (Woman of Valor) is often used as the text for a righteous woman.

How does one select a tombstone today?

Arrangements for a gravestone are made sometime after the *shiva* period has concluded. Usually the funeral director or the rabbi can recommend a monument maker to the family of the deceased. The monument itself is usually made of stone or metal, and is upright or flat. It should of course be dignified and not ostentatious. The rabbi is a good choice of person to help the family select an appropriate verse or review all that will be written on the tombstone.

What is the unveiling?

While there is really no regulation concerning the time

when the tombstone should be erected, it has become customary in North American communities to do so at the end of the year of mourning. The tombstone is consecrated with a brief service called an unveiling, since the custom is to cover the stone with a cloth and have a family member(s) remove it during the ceremony. The unveiling ceremony presents an additional opportunity for the family to pay tribute to the deceased and to speak to the living about the meaning of life and death. Participants should take special care to insure that the unveiling does not become a social event or another funeral.

It is appropriate for the immediate family and close friends and relatives to be invited to the unveiling. Although there often is a rabbi present to officiate, the ceremony is brief and quite simple, and a member of the family, with some rabbinic assistance in advance, can conduct it if they so desire. A typical unveiling might consist of the reading of several Psalms, a few brief remarks and reflections related to the deceased, the removal of the cloth covering the tombstone, and the chanting of the *El Malei Rachamim* prayer. If there are ten adult persons present, the Mourner's Kaddish would also be recited.

It has become customary for each person present to place a small stone on the tombstone at the conclusion of the ceremony. This is our way of acknowledging that we have visited the cemetery.

When and how often does one visit the grave after the year of mourning concludes?

Judaism has always tried to discourage excessive grave visitation. However, there are suggested suitable times to visit graves (and these are the times that are appropriate, too, for an unveiling). Among the most appropriate days for grave visitation are the day that concludes the *sheloshim,* the day of the *yahrzeit,* fast days such as Tisha B'Av, and the whole month of Elul prior to the onset of the High Holidays. Visitations ought not to be made on the Sabbath or on Passover or Sukkot (including their immediate days), or on Shavuot.

What is a yahrzeit?

Yahrzeit is a German or Yiddish word meaning "year's time" and refers to the annual commemoration of a loved one's death. The Talmud mentions a son who fasted on the anniversary of his father's death, and many students in talmudic times visited the graves of their teachers to mark the anniversary of their deaths.

Each year today, on the anniversary of the death of a loved one, a special day is consecrated to that remembrance. It is held on the anniversary of the death according to the Hebrew calendar. If a person does not know the exact date of the death, he should choose a date and from then on observe it as the *Yahrzeit.*

The *Yahrzeit* officially begins with the lighting of a twenty-four hour candle on the night of the anniversary of the death. Light symbolizes a person's soul, and suggests immortality. On the day of the *Yahrzeit,* it is customary to attend services and recite the Mourner's Kaddish. The *El Malei Rachamim* prayer is chanted in memory of the deceased as well. It is also a fitting tribute to the deceased if one can lead the service in his or her honor. On the Sabbath preceding the *Yahrzeit,* it is also a custom to call the mourner to the Torah for an *aliyah.*

Other practices also associated with the commemoration of a Yahrzeit might include Torah study, giving *tzedakah,* visiting the cemetery, and fasting.

What is Yizkor?

Yizkor is a Hebrew word meaning "remembrance" and refers to special memorial services associated with certain Jewish holidays which are specifically devoted to the memory of our loved ones. In Conservative Judaism, *Yizkor* takes place on Yom Kippur, Shemini Atzeret, Passover, and Shavuot.

Yizkor prayers may be said for all Jewish dead: parents, grandparents, husbands and wives, children, family and friends.

The *Yizkor* service itself consists of several biblical passages related to the meaning of life and death, specific passages directed at remembering our loved ones (including Jewish martyrs and those who perished in the Holocaust), the *El Malei Rachamim* prayer and the Mourner's Kaddish. In many Conservative synagogues Psalm 23 ("The Lord is My Shepherd") is also recited.

Some Jewish people follow the custom of leaving the synagogue during the *Yizkor* service if their parents are alive. This practice is based in part upon a superstition that harm might come to their parents if they remained. Many rabbis, however, encourage all people to stay for *Yizkor*, since there are remembrance prayers for martyrs, friends, soldiers, and those who died in the Holocaust.

As with the *Yahrzeit*, it is also customary to kindle a twenty-four hour candle on the evening preceding a *Yizkor* service. Mourners also may want to give *tzedakah* and perform other loving deeds of kindness to honor their loved one's memory.

SPECIAL QUESTIONS AND CONCERNS
RELATED TO DEATH AND DYING

What is the Jewish attitude toward suicide?

Jewish law indicates that there may be no mourning for a person who commits suicide willfully. This means that there is no rending of the clothes, no eulogizing, and so forth, but words of comfort shall be given to the bereaved family. The Jewish people, however, have always been sensitive to the state of mind which would lead any person to commit suicide. Nowadays, since it is known that most cases of suicide result from temporary insanity often caused by depression, all rites of mourning are observed. Also taken into account with regard to any suicide is the fact that any humiliation of the dead adds to the anguish of those already bereaved. Thus, only rarely today are self-inflicted deaths labeled as suicides within the context of Jewish law.

May one be buried in a mausoleum?

Since the requirement to bury the dead refers specifically to burial in the ground, a mausoleum built over a burial plot is permissible. However, mausoleums in which the casket is kept above the earth are contrary to the biblical directive which emphasizes earthly burial.

Vaults are permitted today in those areas where they are required by civil law, usually because of the water table of the land.

Is cremation permissible?

The Jewish way of burial has always been to place the body of the deceased into the earth. The Law Committee of the Rabbinical Assembly has ruled that cremation is of the Rabbinical Assembly has ruled that cremation is not permitted. When it is done by the family in disregard of Jewish practice, a Conservative rabbi may officiate at the funeral service, the ashes may be buried in a Jewish cemetery, and appropriate prayers may be said, but not by the rabbi.

Is embalming permissible?

While there are instances of embalming in the Bible (such as the case of Joseph; Genesis 50:26), the later talmudic authorities forbade the practice, because it infringes upon the respect due to the deceased. Today, for sanitary reasons and sometimes by requirement of civil law, it sometimes becomes necessary to embalm a body. Such cases may be due to a need to delay the burial, as for example, when a body is shipped a long distance or if a person dies at sea.

Is euthanasia permissible?

Euthanasia, from the Greek for "beautiful death" and often referred to as "mercy killing," is forbidden by Jewish law. The issue has become somewhat clouded today because postponing death unnecessarily is also prohibited and even traditional authorities do not agree on what constitutes the active cessation of life. Traditionalists seem to suggest that one is not required to attach any life-prolonging device to a terminally ill patient but may not remove them once attached. There are some Conservative authorities who seem to suggest that such devices may be removed and nature be allowed to take its course. To be safe, it is best for a person to consult his or her rabbinic authority in matters of euthanasia.

What happens to amputated limbs?

If an individual severs his limbs and subsequently dies, the limbs are to be buried with the deceased. Limbs amputated at an earlier time should have been buried in the eventual grave of the individual or in a family plot nearby. The guiding Jewish principle related to amputation of parts is that Jews are to be buried as completely as possible, just as they were born, and that all body parts are made in the image of God.

May organ parts be donated?

Modern medical science today has made it possible to save the eyesight of a living person by transplanting the cornea of the eye of a deceased person and to heal certain diseases by transplanting tissue from another person. Is the mutilation of the corpse necessitated by such procedures to be regarded as desecration of the deceased?

The weight of opinion is that it is not, and that there can be no greater honor to the deceased than to bring healing to the living. It is therefore permissible in Conservative Judaism to will one's eyes or other organs and body tissue for transplantation. The guiding principle here is that of *pikuach nefesh,* saving and extending another's life.

Are autopsies permitted?

It is quite clear from classic Jewish literature that autopsies were performed on occasion and that some rabbis were very familiar with anatomy. Still, an aversion to autopsy was a custom that gradually acquired the status of law.

Today, routine autopsies are forbidden because they violate the principle of honor and respect due to the deceased (*kevod hamet*). An autopsy is permitted, however, in these circumstances:

1. When the physician claims that it could provide new knowledge that would help to cure others suffering from the same disease.
2. When civil law requires it in order to determine the cause of death.

THE WORLD BEYOND THE GRAVE

Judaism as a religion has generally been much more concerned with this world than the next. However, there are a variety of responses related to the question 'What happens after I die?' The following is a brief summary of some of the forms in which our people have conceived of a life after life.

What does the Bible say about an afterlife?

There is in the Bible virtually no intimation of a belief that there is life after death. The Bible does mention a shadowy place called *sheol,* but it is neither described nor defined in any kind of detail. The essential thrust of the Bible is that living life is important and that living a good life will be rewarded in this life, while living a bad life will be punished in this life.

What do the prophets say about an afterlife?

The biblical prophets spoke eloquently of the resurrection. "Your dead shall live," declared Isaiah (26:19). In Ezekiel's vision in the valley of the dry bones (chapter 37), the bones took on flesh and came back to life. According to some of the prophets, there would come a day when a Messiah would come and raise the dead. At that time, the Jews will be restored to the Land of Israel, where a descendant of King David will sit on the throne in a world of peace and tranquility. By the time of the Talmud, this belief had been elaborated into a detailed system of physical resurrection and immortality of the soul.

What do Jewish mystics believe about life after death?

During the Middle Ages, Jewish mystics outlined a new belief in *gilgul hanefesh,* the transmigration of the soul, or reincarnation. The mystics believed that every person has a soul and a task to accomplish on earth. If the task is completed in the course of one's lifetime, the soul returns to God after death. If not, the soul returns to earth again and again in different vessels until its mission is accomplished.

What do Jewish philosophers say about life after death?

Perhaps the most famous rationalist philosopher was the twelfth-century philosopher known as Maimonides. For Maimonides, God is pure intelligence. Therefore, whatever immortality people achieve is through their intellect. The greater the thoughts that people think, the closer they come to God's thoughts and the closer they get to immortality.

What are some other possible forms in which immortality is perceived?

The following is a brief summary of some of the other ways of which immortality is conceived:

1. **Immortality of the soul:** This traditional view, affirmed by Judaism, holds that the body of a person returns to the earth, but the soul returns to God who gave it. The

2. **Influence through family:** Some believe that people live on through their families and descendants. This means that people live on biologically through their children.
3. **Immortality through influence, deeds, and creative works:** This means that people live on through their works, thoughts, and actions, which can continue to influence people even after death.
4. **Influence through memory:** This means that people live on through the memory of those who knew and loved them. Remembering any person provides that person with his or her immortality.

Glossary

Aliyah: The honor of being called to bless the Torah at the time it is being read in the synagogue.

Ashkenazim: Jews who follow the traditions of north and central Europe.

Aufruf: The "calling up" of the groom-to-be (and often the bride-to-be) to the Torah for an *aliyah.*

B.C.E. Before the Common Era

Badeken: Ceremony for veiling the bride.

Bar Mitzvah (for girls: *Bat Mitzvah*): One who is responsible for observing the *mitzvot* (religious acts). For boys this occurs at age thirteen, while for girls this occurs at age twelve.

Bet Din: A court of Jewish law.

Bikkur Cholim: Visiting the sick, an important religious obligation.

Brit Milah: Circumcision.

C.E. Common Era

Chevra Kaddisha: Literally "holy society," this group is responsible for preparing the deceased for burial.

Chol HaMoed: The intermediate days of the Jewish festivals i.e., Sukkot and Passover.

Chuppah: The wedding canopy.

Codes: Books of Jewish law.

Confirmation: Ceremony often tied to festival of Shavuot in which teenagers participate and confirm their acceptance of Judaism.

Erusin: Betrothal.

El Malei Rachamim: Prayer for the peace of the departed soul.

Gemara: Major Rabbinic commentary on the Mishnah, a part of the Talmud.

Ger: A Jewish convert.

Get: A Jewish divorce.

Haftarah: Meaning "conclusion," it is the prophetic section recited after the reading of the Torah on the Sabbath and festivals.

163

Kashrut: The system of Jewish dietary laws.

Keriah: Tearing of the garment as a sign of mourning.

Ketubah: Jewish marriage contract.

Kohen: Descendant from the priestly family.

Kvater/Kvaterin: German-derived words meaning godfather and godmother, appointed at the time of a circumcision.

Mamzer: Child born of a forbidden marriage.

Midrash: Type of rabbinic commentary on the Bible that explains the underlying significance of biblical texts.

Mikvah: A Jewish ritual bath.

Minyan: A quorum of ten persons needed for a prayer service.

Mishnah: First postbiblical code of Jewish law, elaborated upon by the Gemara.

Mitzvah: A religious commandment. Judaism has 613 of them.

Mohel/Mohelet: Person who performs the surgery of circumcision at a *Brit Milah.*

Mourner's Kaddish: Traditional prayer affirming life, recited by mourners.

Nisuin: Marriage

Onen: Mourner prior to the funeral, who is exempted from the performance of religious obligations.

Passover: Jewish spring festival commemorating the exodus of the Jews from Egyptian slavery.

Pidyon HaBen: Ceremony for the redemption of the firstborn.

Rabbinical Assembly: Professional organization for Conservative rabbis.

Responsa: Written replies given to questions on all aspects of Jewish law by qualified authorities.

Rosh Chodesh: Beginning of a new Jewish month.

Sandek: Person honored with the duty of holding the baby boy at the *Brit Milah* ceremony.

Sephardim: Jews who practice the traditions which grew up in Spain and North Africa.

Seudat Mitzvah: Festive meal following a Jewish life cycle event or other ritual occasion.

Seventeenth of Tammuz: Day in the Hebrew month of Tammuz on

which traditional Jews fast. It commemorates the beginning of the downfall of Jerusalem in 586 B.C.E.

Shadchan: Jewish matchmaker or marriage broker.

Shavuot: Jewish spring festival (seven weeks after Passover) commemorating both the spring harvest and the receiving of the Ten Commandments on Mount Sinai.

Shalom Zachar/Nekevah: Ceremony welcoming a new born boy or girl, usually held the Friday evening before the Brit Milah ceremony.

Sheloshim: The first thirty days of the mourning period.

Shemini Atzeret: Jewish festival celebrated after Sukkot. On it *Yizkor* Memorial prayers are recited.

Sheva Berachot: Seven wedding blessings.

Shulchan Aruch: Authoritative code of Jewish law written by Joseph Karo in the sixteenth century.

Shiva: Literally "seven," it refers to the first seven days of mourning.

Simcha: Joyous occasion.

Taharah: Ritual cleansing of the deceased by the *Chevra Kaddish* prior to the funeral.

Talmud: Compendium of Jewish law, consisting of the Mishnah and the Gemara.

Tenaim: Stipulations concerning a proposed marriage.

Torah: The five books of Moses: Genesis, Exodus, Leviticus, Numbers, and Deuteronomy.

Unveiling: Service marking the consecration of a tombstone.

Vidui: Jewish confessional prayer.

Yahrzeit: Anniversary of the death of an individual.

Yizkor: Memorial prayers recited on Shemini Atzeret, Passover, Shavuot, and Yom Kippur.

Bibliography

Diamant, Anita. The Jewish Baby Book. Summit Books, 1988.

——. The New Jewish Wedding. Summit Books, 1985.

Donin, Hayim HaLevy. To Be a Jew. Basic Books, 1972.

Gold, Michael. And Hannah Wept: Infertility, Adoption and the Jewish Couple. Jewish Publication Society, 1988.

Gordis, Robert. Understanding Conservative Judaism. Rabbinical Assembly, 1978.

Guggenheimer, Heinrich W. Jewish Family Names and their Origins: An Etymological Dictionary. Ktav Publishing House, Inc., 1992.

Isaacs, Ronald. The Bride and Groom Handbook. Behrman House, 1988.

Isaacs, Ronald H., and Olitzky, Kerry M. A Jewish Mourner's Handbook. Ktav Publishing House, Inc., 1992.

Klein, Isaac. A Guide to Jewish Religious Practice (augmented edition) Jewish Theological Seminary, 1992.

Kolatch, Alfred J. The Name Dictionary. Jonathan David, 1967.

Levine, Elizabeth Resnick (editor). A Ceremonies Sampler: New Rites, Celebrations, and Observances of Jewish Women. Woman's Institute for Continuing Jewish Education, 1991.

Romanoff, Lena. Your People, My People: Finding Acceptance and Fulfillment as a Jew by Choice. Jewish Publication Society, 1990.

Siegel, Seymour, and Gertel, Elliot (editors). God in the Teachings of Conservative Judaism. Rabbinical Assembly, 1985.

Siegel, Seymour (editor). Conservative Judaism and Jewish Law. Rabbinical Assembly, 1977.

Waxman, Mordecai (editor). Tradition and Change: The Development of Conservative Judaism. Burning Bush Press, 1970.

RITES OF PASSAGE:

A Guide to the Jewish Life Cycle

Ronald H. Isaacs

KTAV Publishing House, Inc.
Hoboken, New Jersey

Manufactured in the United States of America